Designing Patchwork

ON YOUR COMPUTER

Designing
Patchwork
ON YOUR COMPUTER

CAROL PHILLIPSON

krause publications
An imprint of F+W Publications, Inc.

©2007 The Ilex Press Ltd.

Published by

kp krause publications

An imprint of F+W Publications, Inc.

700 East State Street • Iola, WI 54990-0001
715-445-2214 • 888-457-2873
www.krause.com

Our toll-free number to place an order or obtain
a free catalog is (800) 258-0929.

This book was conceived, designed, and produced by
The Ilex Press Limited, Lewes, England

Library of Congress Catalog Number: 2006934230

Designers: Jane & Chris Lanaway
Editor: Adam Juniper

ISBN 13: 978-0-89689-400-6
ISBN 10: 0-89689-400-2

Printed in China

Contents

6   Introduction

12   **Computer Basics**

14   Using your computer for designs

18   Essential functions

22   Creating your own grids

26   Customizing colors

28   **Patchwork Projects**

30   Rainbow Squares

32   Courthouse Square

34   Seven-Patch Bear's Paw Quilt

38   Sashing and Borders

42   Designing a quilt using borders

46   Basket Wall Hanging

52   Log Cabin Poppy Quilt

60   Scrappy Herring-Bone Wall Hanging

64   Star Wall Hanging

70   Designing a Hexagon Wall Hanging

76   Baby Quilt or Playmat

78   Foundation piecing

80   Foundation-pieced Seasons Hanging

84   Countryside Quilt

92   Christmas Hanging

96   Crazy Patchwork

102   Printing onto fabric

104   Flower Quilt

112   Diamond Wedding Hanging

122   Individual quilt labels

126   Index

128   Acknowledgments

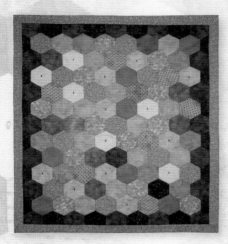

Introduction

It is interesting to me that, even in the 21st century, the old crafts of patchwork and quilting are still popular, even though the necessity of using every available scrap of fabric to keep warm has somewhat diminished. In many countries throughout the world, patchworkers and quilters spend numerous hours designing and stitching.

Nowadays, when there is such a widespread use of computers for both business and pleasure, it seems only sensible to make use of their versatility to give a helping hand with original quilt designs. An amazing amount can be achieved with only a basic graphics program like Microsoft Paint, by following this book's simple instructions.

Not everyone has the space to have a full-size "design wall" where they can pin up the pieces of a quilt to assess the design. The computer screen, however, can successfully replace the design wall. It gives you the chance to quickly and easily plan your patchwork so you gain a clear impression of just how the completed quilt will look. You can iron out anomalies in your design, change the colors, reposition the blocks, add sashing and borders—or erase them—before a single stitch is made. This avoids wasted time, fabric, and patience! Although more time is created to actually sew, be warned—designing quilts on the computer can be addictive!

Countryside quilt
This design illustrates how easy it is to use your computer to create designs which are made up of a variety of different block sizes.

You only need a very basic understanding of computers to be able to follow these step-by-step stages in planning a quilt, yet there is plenty of creative scope, keeping the more experienced "computer quilters" happy too.

The techniques learned from this book will enable you to create individual quilt designs, which, alongside your personal choice of fabrics and finishing, will produce unique quilts.

Techniques and Tips on Designing a Quilt

As there are many excellent detailed books on patchwork and this book is primarily concerned with using a computer to design patchwork blocks and quilts, I shall mainly deal with the specific techniques that are relevant to the book.

Patchwork is the sewing together, by hand or machine, of pieces of fabric to create a design. This may be traditional blocks or modern free designs. Most of the designs included in the book are the former, but the procedures learned can be applied to developing free designs and appliqué. Patchwork doesn't have to entail the purchase of masses of equipment, but of course there are, as with any hobby, many "extras" or "essentials" that can be purchased to make life easier.

Planning a quilt

Using the computer to plan a quilt gives a lot of flexibility because the design can be easily changed until you are happy with the result. Follow the steps on the following pages to plan your quilt.

Designing on a computer
The Prairie Star Medallion quilt design (top) is typical of those that have a single central motif. The Square 4-Patch design (center) is typical of a "strippy quilt." Notice the sashing and borders of the strippy design.

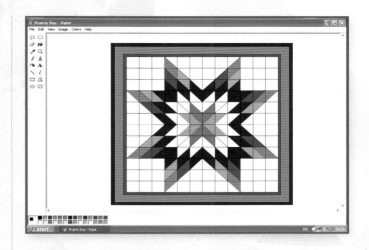

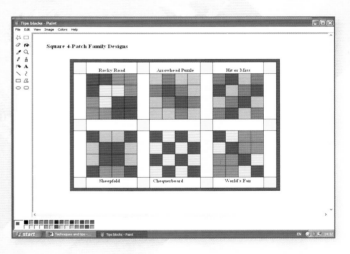

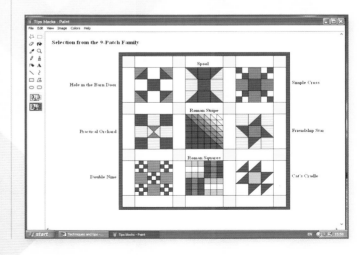

Choosing the block or blocks

A block is a single pieced, appliquéd, or quilted unit, generally square. The first step in creating a block is to decide which pattern is to be used. Often the whole quilt will be stitched using a traditional block design that is already established.

The individual shapes that form the larger blocks fall roughly into four basic groups: squares, rectangles, triangles, and curves. In addition there are hexagons and octagons and many blocks with mixed shapes. Blocks can be pieced using one or a combination of any of these. A quilt may be simply made up of a single repetitive block, or have several repetitive blocks that create secondary patterns, or be a sampler quilt using lots of different blocks.

Quilts with one central motif, generally surrounded by borders, are known as Medallion quilts. Quilts in strips with sashing and borders between are known, appropriately, as "strippy quilts." The center panels of these may either be pieced, or just be a strip of printed fabric.

Squares and rectangles are the easiest to work with and to design using a grid on the computer. However, within the book you will be guided through the construction of designs using many other shapes.

Squares, rectangles, and triangles are drawn on a grid of squares, the most common being a nine-patch; i.e. three squares by three squares. Of course, this can then be divided into blocks of six-by-six, nine-by-nine, and so on. Similarly, four-patch grids can progress to eight-by-eight or 16-by-16. Blocks in the same patch family will mix and match as they are drawn to the same-size block.

Some designs cannot be broken down into square blocks. These are frequently pieced from patches of the same size and shape and are known as one-patch designs. An example of this is the Rainbow Quilt, also known as the Thousand Pyramids, which is made of different color triangular patches; another example is the Herringbone quilt, which is based on parallelograms—although in this quilt, squares have been added. Like the Trip Around The World, these can be created to any size repeating the same shape.

The one-patch Trip Around The World quilt can grow ad infinitum.

The Rainbow Squares and Herringbone quilts are also one-patch designs.

Rainbow Squares

Herringbone

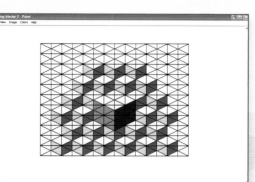

Similar tones
The similar tones of color in this Hexagon Hanging have a calm and serene effect.

Complementary colors
This Log Cabin quilt design uses colors that are directly opposite each other on the color wheel.

Color wheel
The color wheel is a useful device to keep track of color effects. The large segments [p] are the primary colors, and the middle segments [s] between each large segment are secondary colors.

Thinking about color
Once you have chosen the block or blocks, they can be duplicated and arranged quickly and efficiently using the computer. After that, colors need to be added, and the beauty of doing this on the computer is that you can experiment with as many different variations as you like without having to start all over again each time. Try swapping dark and light colors, or try the same design with graduated colors. Even after colors are applied, neighboring blocks can be flipped or rotated as you please.

Placing certain colors adjacent to others can change the overall impression of a quilt. Look at the color wheel above to help you plan which colors to use. The colors opposite each other on the color wheel are called complementary colors. These, like purple and yellow, or red and green (as used in the Log Cabin quilt on page 52, a sample of which is shown above), provoke a lively reaction, whereas colors that sit adjacent or close together on the wheel, like blue and violet or blue and green (as used in the Hexagon quilt shown at the top of the page) appear softer and more harmonious.

Color warmth
When a cool color like blue or green is adjacent to a warm color like red, orange, or yellow, the warm color appears farther forward, and the cool color recedes. In the same way, lighter colors seem to be nearer the front of the design than darker ones. Applying these theories can help when you want to add a three-dimensional look to your design.

This color theory can be applied to liven up a quilt that seems to be lacking in contrast, or it can soothe a design that is too busy. Adding a few splashes of yellow to a mainly purple quilt will bring it to life. The same effect can be seen in the orange squares used in the computer design of the blue-pieced sashing on page 38.

Exchanging some complementary colors for colors that sit closer together on the color wheel will bring more unity to a fragmented design.

Planning the layout of the blocks

Arrangements for the placement of multiple blocks are called settings. Changing these makes the appearance of the block seem very different.

Ask yourself if the blocks are to be arranged horizontally or diagonally ("on-point"), like the Courthouse Square design on page 32. Are they going to be next to each other, or will they alternate with other blocks?

Try lots of ideas on the computer before selecting the one to stitch. It is surprising how the appearance of the design changes.

Secondary patterns

Secondary patterns may occur when using certain designs, as with the Blue Star and Hole in One blocks. Any patterns formed become clearer if the alternating design is not colored. Use your computer's *Select > Edit > **Copy***, and *Edit > **Paste*** functions to experiment.

Alternating

Note the secondary pattern formed by alternating the Blue Star block and the Hole in One block.

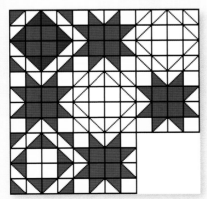

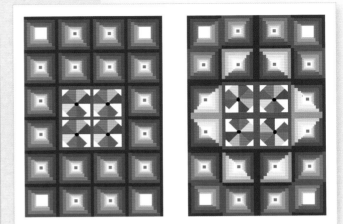

Alternative designs

The final design worked out on the computer for the Poppy Log Cabin quilt on page 52 was very different from my original plan.

Planning sashing

Plans for sashing and/or borders can be worked out easily using the computer. It offers a very simple way of experimenting, enabling lots of different options to be viewed before a final decision is made.

Sashing bands are strips of fabric running between the individual blocks. They frame the block, giving it a latticed look. The strips can either be horizontal and vertical, framing a square block, or diagonal, to surround "on-point" blocks.

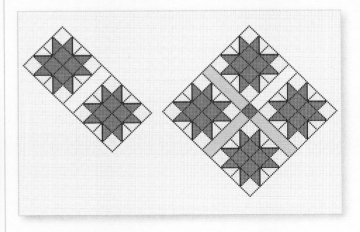

Sashing strips

Sashing strips can either be plain or pieced, but in both cases are used to separate the individual blocks.

To form sashing strips on the computer, select and drag two blocks from the design, positioning them in line but leaving a gap between them, then use the Line tool to fill the ends in, forming an enclosed unit, before choosing a color and applying it to the strip with the Fill with Color tool.

Experiment with the spacing of the blocks. Do the blocks look better next to each other as in the Log Cabin Poppy quilt? Or with sashing between, like the Basket Quilt on page 46? Does it look better with a wide or narrow sashing? Are there to be sashing squares at the intersections like on the Bear's Paw quilt on page 34?

The next step, when the quilt center is complete, is to design the border, another skill altogether, and one which we consider later in the book, starting on page 40.

Repeat and experiment

The computer gives you the opportunity to experiment with sashing, and the style you eventually choose will have a big effect on how your blocks work with each other.

Vertical or horizontal?

Notice how the vertical and horizontal sashing on the strippy quilt and small hanging displays the star blocks.

Creating half-square triangles

Many quilt designs, such as the Rainbow Square quilt, have half-square triangles in their composition. Once you have a plan to work from, and can see which units are needed for the quilt, an easy way to create half-square triangles is to cut whole squares from each of the two colors that will form the triangular half-square. The sides of these two squares should be the side length of the finished triangle with $\frac{7}{8}$-inch added. For example, if the short sides of the triangle need to measure two inches, cut two squares measuring $2\frac{7}{8}$-inches. Place the squares together with right sides facing and draw a diagonal line across one of the squares. Using this line as a guide, stitch a $\frac{1}{4}$-inch line either side of it. Cut along the line and you will have two half-square triangles ready to use in your design.

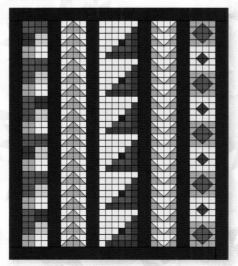

Traditional borders

This design, which we'll learn more about on page 42, is composed entirely of traditional border patterns.

Computer Basics

Using your computer for designs

These days computers come in all shapes and sizes, but for the most part they are from only two different stables. The vast majority run some form of Microsoft's Windows operating system, while the distinctive Apple Macintosh systems remain more popular with some. From the patchworker's point of view, the only difference is that Windows includes a program—Paint—which is well suited to our needs. Here is how to find it or, if you're using a Macintosh, where to get hold of an alternative.

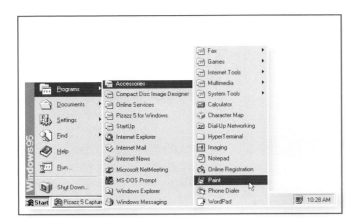

Windows 95, 98, or Me

Windows 95 and 98 have a gray Start button in the bottom-left corner with the word "Start" written on it. In the 95 edition, click *Start > Accessories > **Paint*** to open the Paint program. In Windows 98 you'll need to click *Start > Programs > Accessories > **Paint***.

Windows XP

By default, Windows XP has a green Start button on a blue Taskbar. Click on the Start button—if you use Paint regularly it may appear at the top of the first menu which appears, in which case simply select it. If not, you'll need to click on *All Programs > Accessories > **Paint*** to launch the program.

Windows Vista

The new Windows Vista interface takes the text away from the Start button, but it still serves a similar function. Click on it and follow the menu to *Programs > Accessories > **Paint***.

Mac OS X

Apple computers are distinct from nearly all PCs in that they use their own operating system, called Mac OS X. Just as Windows has developed over the years, Mac OS X has come in several versions, called 10.0, 10.1, and so on. These are often known by their codenames, which have so far all been big cats (Cheetah, Puma, Jaguar, Panther, Tiger, Leopard). No version so far has included an equivalent of Microsoft Paint, so if you are using any of these operating systems, you'll need to find an alternative.

Though there are some freeware (software you can download from the internet for free) and shareware (software that costs a small amount) solutions available, none of them are perfect. At the time of writing, Seashore (http://seashore.sourceforge.net) seems promising, though since it has no tool for drawing straight lines, you would have to rely solely on the grids supplied on the CD.

Another option is Adobe Photoshop Elements, a sophisticated image editor available for Mac or PC. As well as offering an exciting array of tools to play around with your digital photos (another hobby you might want to take up), Photoshop Elements also has equivalents to all the tools in Microsoft Paint. You can download a 30-day trial version from www.adobe.com (there are on-screen instructions to install it). The basic equivalent tools are shown here (the Paint tools are introduced over the page).

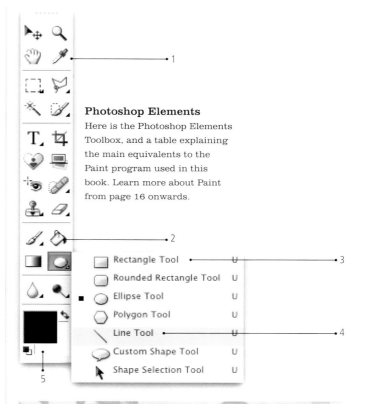

Photoshop Elements

Here is the Photoshop Elements Toolbox, and a table explaining the main equivalents to the Paint program used in this book. Learn more about Paint from page 16 onwards.

Rectangle Tool	U
Rounded Rectangle Tool	U
Ellipse Tool	U
Polygon Tool	U
Line Tool	U
Custom Shape Tool	U
Shape Selection Tool	U

Apple iMac
Modern computers all work in a similar way, with a mouse click used to access menus.

1 Eyedropper tool Use this instead of the Pick Color tool in Paint.

2 Paint Bucket tool The paint bucket will pour the presently selected color at the point clicked. Ensure that the Contiguous option (at the top of the screen) is selected.

3 Rectangular Selection tool Use this tool instead of Paint's Select tool; it works in the same way.

4 Line tool The Line tool is located in a group of shape tools; to reveal these sub menus, click and hold on any tool with a black mark to the bottom right.

5 Foreground color This is the presently selected color which will be applied to the page if you use the Line, Brush, or other tools.

Color Swatches In addition to the Toolbox, Photoshop Elements has additional windows (called "palettes") for certain jobs. By clicking *Window > Color Swatches*, you bring up a simple color key tool. Click the New Color Swatch at the bottom to add a new color, and load or save your own personal swatches via the More button.

Basic computer tools and functions

Whichever graphics program you are using, the first step toward using this book successfully is to identify the basic functions that are referred to throughout. The images in this book are from the basic graphics program Paint, which is included with most versions of Microsoft Windows (see page 14). If you are using a different program, locate the tools in your program that are equivalent to those indicated on the diagram below. In many applications, if you move the mouse pointer slowly over an icon, a brief description of its function will appear.

Menu bar

Situated along the top of the screen, below the title bar, is a Menu bar. this contains menus for changing and manipulating a design. Each menu contains a group of related commands. To open a menu, either click once on the name if you are using the mouse, or hold down Alt or F10 and type the key that corresponds to the underlined letter in the menu name. Some of the menu commands have keyboard shortcut commands and these are given next to the name. For instance, the Flip and Rotate box can be brought up by pressing Ctrl+R; that is, holding the Ctrl key down and tapping the R key once before releasing both keys.

Tools

At the left side of the screen is the Toolbar or Toolbox. This contains icons or small pictures that represent each tool. These can be selected by one left-click on the mouse. To view the function of each tool, move the cursor slowly over the icon and its name will appear. When an icon is selected, an Options box may appear below the Toolbox to give you more choice.

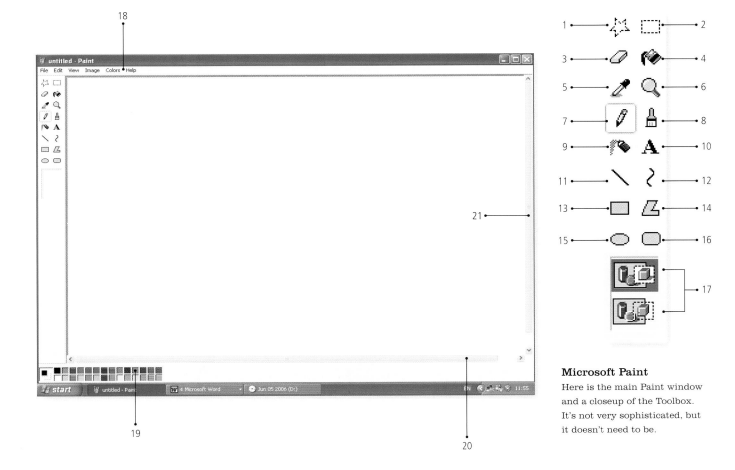

Microsoft Paint

Here is the main Paint window and a closeup of the Toolbox. It's not very sophisticated, but it doesn't need to be.

Microsoft Paint Explained

1. Free-Form Select Allows you to outline an precise area to change.

2. Select This selects part of a picture or design to be worked on by enclosing it within straight edges. Point and drag the cursor to enclose the required area and release. A box surrounds the selected area. This allows work in this area to have functions performed on it while the rest of the pattern remains unaffected. To delete the box, click outside it.

3. Eraser Clicking on the Eraser brings up an Option box below the tool icons which allows you to choose the size of the rubber. For the purposes of this book, always choose the smallest size—one pixel wide.

4. Fill With Color Use this to fill an object or line with color. Click a color from the Color Selection box at the bottom of the toolbar, place the paint-pot pointer above the area to be filled, and left-click. If there are any breaks in the unit border, the color will not be restricted to this area and will spread into the drawing area. Edit > Undo will clear it. Zoom in to find and fill in the gap. Right-click to erase a colored area or line.

5. Pick Color Use this to copy a color from another area. It is like an eyedropper. Imagine it sucking up the color then releasing it with the Fill with Color paint-pot. Place the tool over the required color and left-click. The current drawing color in the Color selection box at the bottom will change to the new color and you can then use it elsewhere in your design.

6. Magnifier When you click the magnifying glass, options appear in the Option box for you to select the required magnification. Another box appears to enable you to choose the area to be magnified when the pointer is over the screen. However, for the purposes of working through this book, I suggest you use the View > Zoom option from the Menu bar instead.

7. Pencil Use this to draw a free-form shape, not a straight line. Click on the icon, drag the pointer to form the line, and release.

8. Brush This tool can paint to an area of several pixels at once. It is not used in this book.

9. Airbrush Just as with the Brush tool, this applies color over an area near the mouse, but this time with texture. Again, its use is limited in this book.

10. Text To add text to a piece of work, click the Text tool. The cursor changes to a cross. Drag the cross across the screen to form a box in the position where you want the text. A Fonts box will appear allowing you to select the type and size of font. Choose the size and font and then type the text in the box, then click outside the box to close it. Use Select and drag to move a piece of text.

11. Line tool For drawing straight lines. This is used extensively throughout this book. Click on the icon. In the Option box below the Toolbar, select the width of line that you require. For most projects in the book you need the thinnest line—one pixel thick.

Point the tool at one end of the desired line, drag it to the other end and release. A straight line will form between the two points. If the line is not exactly horizontal, vertical, or at a 45° angle, the computer adjusts it accordingly.

To delete a line, right-click on one end of the line, drag to the other, and release. The line disappears.

12. Curved Line tool This allows you to draw a smooth curve. Choose a line width and draw a line as previously and release. Click on the line where you want the curve to be, drag the pointer to adjust the curve, and release. You are able to have two curves on each line. If you are satisfied with the first curve, click off the screen to prevent the second curve forming. Edit > Undo to delete.

13. Rectangle tool This tool allows you to draw a rectangle by simply clicking and dragging from one corner to another.

14. Polygon tool The polygon tool allows you to draw any shape you like by clicking at each corner point and double-clicking to finish.

15. Ellipse/Circle tool Clicking the icon brings up an option box. The projects in this book require only the simple outline shape and only require you to draw circles. Imagine the circle to be inside a square outline. Drag the pointer from the top left corner diagonally to the bottom right and release. For a perfect circle, hold down the Shift key as you drag the pointer across.

16. Rounded Rectangle tool This tool works in the same way as the Rectangle tool, but—as the name implies—adds rounded corners.

17. Option box These icons change depending on which tool is selected. Here the selected (top) option shows that if a selection were made (dotted line), it could be used to move all the enclosed pixels rather than just the non-white ones.

18. Menu bar The menu options. Click once to make a menu appear and again to choose a menu option.

19. Color Selection box This palette allows you to change the selected color simply by clicking on your choice of new color.

20. Horizontal scroll bar Drag this to move the visible area of the image.

21. Vertical scroll bar Drag this to move the visible area of the image.

Essential Functions

Knowing where the tools are (*see page 16*) is one thing, but using them to your advantage is quite another. Over the next few pages, all the main skills required for the projects in this book will be introduced, drawing attention to the computer's benefits over more traditional techniques.

Cut, Copy & Paste

Cut, Copy, and Paste allow you to make copies of, or to cut out, a selected part of a design. This is great for repeating patterns.

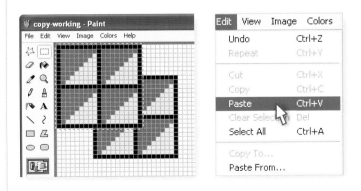

3 Using Copy the outline will disappear but the shape will be still be stored on the virtual "clipboard." (If you choose Cut the selected area will disappear, but will be stored on the clipboard.) When something else replaces the stored image or the computer is turned off, the information is lost.

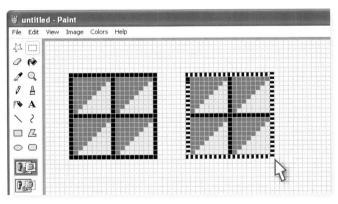

1 To select the area to be copied or cut, first click on the Select tool. The cursor changes to an upright cross. Drag it to enclose the area you wish to copy or cut.

2 When you release the mouse, the selected area will be outlined. Go to *Edit > Copy* or *Edit > Cut*, then click anywhere outside the selected area.

4 Click *Edit > Paste*. An outlined copy will appear on the screen.

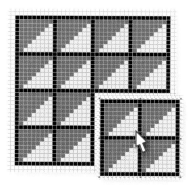

5 Drag this to the required position. You can keep dragging it to adjust it, and then click off the outlined area to release. Remember *Edit > Undo* will clear a mistake. The selected design will stay on the clipboard until something replaces it or the computer is closed down, so any number of copies can be pasted onto the screen.

Transparent or Opaque

When copying, you can choose whether to have the background of the selected area opaque (1) or transparent (2) either by clicking on the boxes at the bottom of the Toolbar or by going to *Image > Draw Opaque*. A transparent background leaves the pattern beneath the background of the selected area visible, while choosing opaque means that the existing pattern will be covered by the background of the selected area.

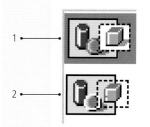

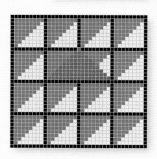

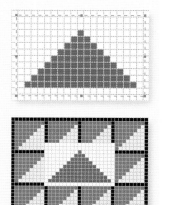

Zooming In, Zooming Out, and Acquiring a Grid

In order to work on a design more easily it will be necessary to magnify sections of the area. Also, the smaller sizes are not large enough to support a grid, so when using Paint, the screen must be at least four times the normal size, i.e. 400%. Some graphics programs will offer a grid under View options.

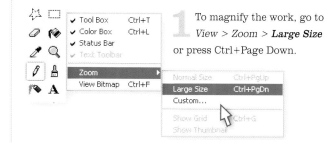

1 To magnify the work, go to *View > Zoom > Large Size* or press Ctrl+Page Down.

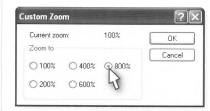

2 For a greater magnification, go to *View > Zoom > Custom* and then choose an option from 200%, 400%, 600%, or 800%. Press OK. (A grid can be obtained only above 400%.)

3 To return to normal size, either press Ctrl+Page Up or *View > Zoom > Normal Size*. If the screen is empty, it will not seem to change, but as soon as you start working, the magnification will be obvious.

400%

600%

800%

Acquiring a grid

To acquire a grid, either press Ctrl+G or *View > Zoom > Show Grid*. To remove a grid, either Press Ctrl+G or *View > Zoom > Show Grid* again.

Saving

It is important to save your work at frequent intervals. These files are too big to save onto a floppy disc, so they need either to be saved directly onto the computer, or onto a CD.

1 To save a new design for the first time, use *File > **Save As***. (Once a design has been saved, the saved version of the file can be updated either by pressing Ctrl+S or *File > **Save***.) A dialog box will appear requiring you to input two pieces of information; the name you want to give to the file, and the place where it is to be saved.

2 A list of places will appear. Make your choice—I usually save my working designs in "My Pictures" then transfer the final ones to a CD, but they may also be saved in "My Documents"—then click the Save button. Here I'll demonstrate the extra steps for saving to CD.

3 At this point, if you have chosen to save directly onto the computer, the file will be written instantaneously and the Save As box will disappear. You can also check that it has been saved by clicking on your desktop and then exploring your files. However, if the work is being saved to a CD, a message will appear letting you know that there are files waiting to be written to the CD.

Saving tip

It is more efficient, in terms of disc space, to save several files using the method in step 3, then only physically burn the files to the CD (steps 4 and 5) at the end of your session on the computer.

4 Click on the balloon from step three. Another box appears showing what is already on the CD and files ready to be written to the CD. The latter will have an arrow on the icon. Click on the ones to be put onto the CD and a highlighted box will show that they have been selected.

5 Go to *File > **Write these files to CD*** and a box will appear. Click Next and another box will let you know how long it will take. When the process is complete, the icon will disappear from the CD Drive box. Close this by clicking on the **✗** as usual.

Opening a saved file

To open a saved design, first open Paint then go to *File > Open*, select from the Look In box the place where the file is saved, scroll down, and click on the correct file name.

Printing and Changing the Size of the Worksheet

Any type of printer, from the latest photo printers to an old dot matrix, can be used—as long as it is compatible with, and set up for, your computer. Getting this right can be a little tricky; the zoom setting on the screen doesn't affect the size on the page. Instead you need to use some other settings.

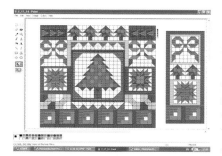

1 When your design is complete, you might find that it doesn't make very efficient use of the page space, leaving a large white area to the bottom right (notice the scroll bars). Working from the very top left, choose the Selection tool and click and drag to select the area you want to keep (allow a small margin), but don't release the mouse button.

2 Before releasing the button, look in the lower-right corner of Paint's window; you'll see some dimensions (for example 940 × 591). Remember these.

3 Now click *Image* > **Attributes** and look at the information box. In the Units section, choose Pixels, then type the dimensions from the last step into the Width and Height boxes and click OK. This trims the wasted space.

4 Click *File* > **Page Setup**. Check that the paper size is correct for your printer, then towards the lower right of the window choose the Fit to option in the Scaling pane. Be sure that both pages are set at 1.

5 If your design is wider than it is tall, click the Landscape option. The gray preview on the left of the window shows what proportion of the page your design will take up. Click OK.

6 To check everything is going according to plan, click *File* > **Print Preview**. This will bring up a window with a representation of where your image will appear on a page if printed with the settings you have selected. If you are happy, click on the Print button (towards to top left).

7 Finally you will be invited to make any printer-specific choices. These depend on what kind of printer you have, but include things like economy mode (for cheaper printing at lower quality). Make your favorite choices and click OK.

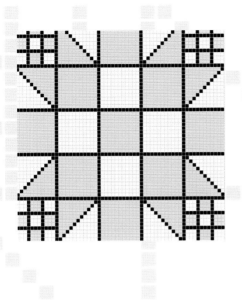

Creating your own grids

When designing patchwork blocks, or indeed a complete quilt, a computer is valuable in two ways. Firstly it can become your "design wall," a space to explore your ideas using the computer to see the whole design and change it easily. Secondly, where required, it can create accurate templates to be used in foundation piecing. In either case, you will need to create an accurate grid. To save you time, all the grids in this book are available—blank or colored—on the supplied CD. Their names are shown on the same page as each project; to access them, simply click *File > Open* and choose the appropriate name.

Designing grids for blocks or quilts

As the viewing area on the computer is not even close to the size of a single, let alone a king-size bed, a basic grid (one smaller than an accurately sized grid) needs to be used, to allow a complete design to be viewed at once. Using this when stitching the actual quilt, one grid square can represent any size you like, maybe one, three, or even 12 inches. If you choose not to use the supplied templates, this is how to create a basic grid in Paint, which is large enough to work on, but can be made smaller to allow you to see a full quilt design. This method can be used to create blocks for any other quilt, including "on-point" designs.

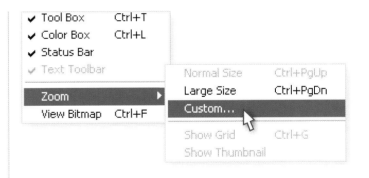

1 Open Paint. Click on *View > Zoom > Custom*. Choose a scale of at least 400%—I usually use 600% or 800%—then click OK. Press Ctrl+G or click on *View > Zoom > Show Grid* and a grid will fill the screen. Each square represents one pixel, so a line of colored squares on 100% or Normal size will appear as a normal line.

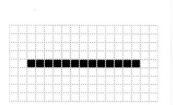

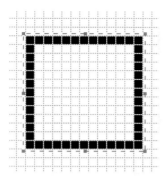

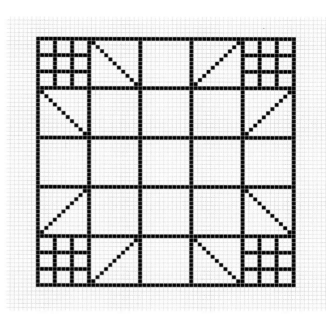

2 Select the Line tool (✎) from the Toolbox and the color black from the palette. Click on a blank square (or "pixel") near the top left of the page to begin drawing, then click on another, 13 pixels along, to draw the line.

3 Draw the other three lines in exactly the same way to make the original line part of a square. Switch to the Select tool (⬚), then click in the top left pixel, drag the mouse to the bottom right and release the button. This selects the square.

6 With black still selected as the foreground color, you can using the Line tool (✎) and black to sub-divide the grid squares to form the pattern. If you have decided each square will be 2 inches, the overall size would be 10 × 10 inches. If each square represented as 2½ inches, the block would be 12½ inches, and so on.

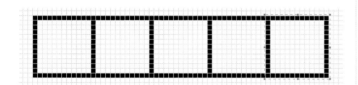

4 Now choose Edit > **Copy** from the menu, followed immediately by Edit > **Paste**. A duplicate square will appear; click on it and move it over the original so that the line overlaps; paste three more times and position to create a row of five squares. (This might be easier using Transparent mode – see page 19.)

7 The design now needs to be colored. Choose a color from the color box to match your intended fabric and click on it to select it (if the colors are not to your taste, you can customize them—see page 24).

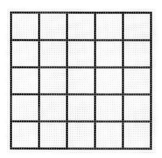

5 Now select the whole row and copy and paste it four times, just as before. This can of course be repeated indefinitely until the required size of grid is achieved, in this case 5 (large squares across) × 5 (large squares down) × 11 (number of pixels between the black lines).

How to Create an Accurate Grid

Many graphics programs, including Photoshop Elements (see page 15), have accurate ruler features supplied. Paint does not, so here is a solution to work around it, should you wish to create grids the same size as the final quilt:

Attributes

File last saved: Not Available
Size on disk: Not Available
Resolution: 85 x 85 dots per inch

Width: 2   Height: 2

Units
⊙ Inches   ○ Cm   ○ Pixels

Colors
○ Black and white   ⊙ Colors

OK
Cancel
Default

1. In Paint, click *Image > Attributes*. Start by typing in the size of a single square in your finished grid—in this case I'm making a 3 × 3 grid with squares of 2 inches, so I type 2 into both the Width and Height boxes and choose Inches, before clicking OK.

Attributes

File last saved: Not Available
Size on disk: Not Available
Resolution: 85 x 85 dots per inch

Width: 6.   Height: 6

Units
⊙ Inches   ○ Cm   ○ Pixels

Colors
○ Black and white   ⊙ Colors

OK
Cancel
Default

3. With the lines drawn, click *Image > Attributes* again and type in the final dimensions of your grid in Inches, in this case 6 (2 × 3 inch squares).

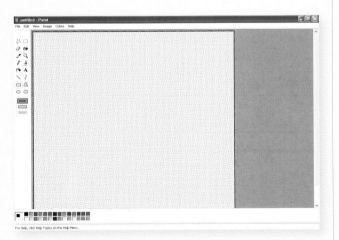

2. Now draw a black rectangle around the exact edge of the image area, using the same tools as normal.

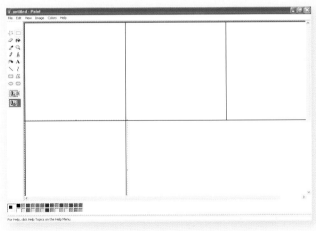

4. Finally, copy and paste your original square as before.

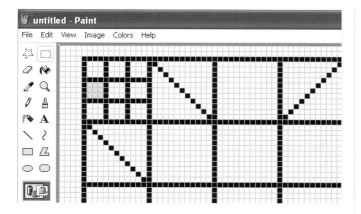

8 The selected color (to the left of the color box) will change to reflect your choice in the last step. Now, select the Fill With Color tool (🖌) to select a color, then point the cursor to the area to be filled and left-click. The color will fill up to the surrounding lines (it stops because they are a different color, so it's best never to use black).

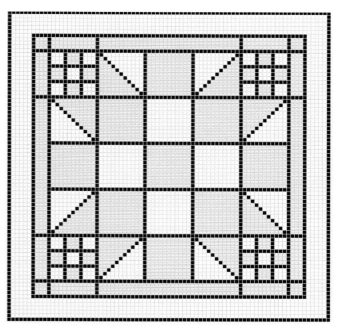

10 To add a plain border, choose black from the color box, then select the Rectangle tool (▭) (be sure to choose its Outline option). Now click and drag with the mouse, as with the Select tool, from a pixel above and left of the grid to one equally far right and below it. You can fill this border as before, add another, or switch to the Line tool (◣) to divide it into smaller patches.

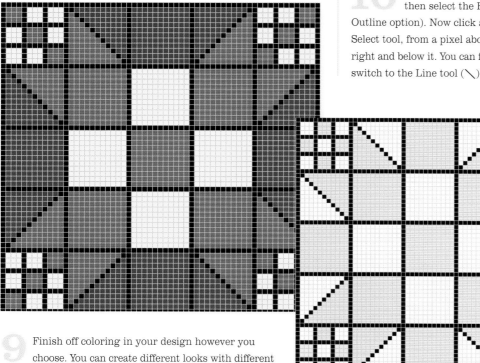

9 Finish off coloring in your design however you choose. You can create different looks with different colors, which is why the computer is such a useful tool.

Customizing Colors

You can color your design by left-clicking one of the colors in the Color box and using the *Fill With Color* tool, but to give a more accurate representation of your design, you can customize the colors to match those of your fabrics.

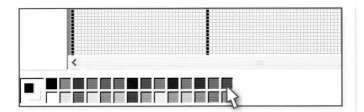

1 First, click on the color that you want to change in the Color box. Do not change the black, white, or gray on the left-hand side, as these are the drawing, background, and grid colors. I have chosen the top right box to change.

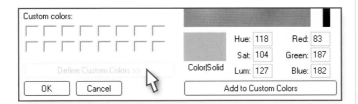

2 Click *Colors* > **Edit Colors**. A box appears containing the same colors as in the color box at the bottom of the screen. Click *Define Custom Colors*. The color screen expands, adding a variegated color box with a black marker, and, at the side of this, a thin color column with a slider.

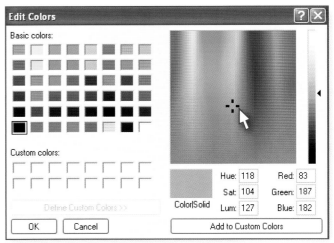

3 To choose the correct range of color to match your fabric, either select the nearest color from the left-hand Basic color box, or click and move the black marker to the appropriate color area on the variegated box. You will notice that the color range in the column to the right of the box will change. Left-click and move the slider to the nearest shade, then click *Add to Custom Colors*. The color of your choice will appear in one of the empty Custom Color boxes.

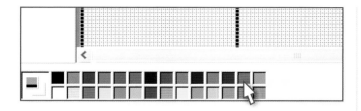

4 Click OK. The Color box on the main screen that you selected will fill with your last chosen color and the Edit Colors box will disappear. In the Color box, select another color to change. Click *Colors* > **Edit Colors**. Choose another of the colors that you customized, press *OK*. The box will have filled with your color choice.

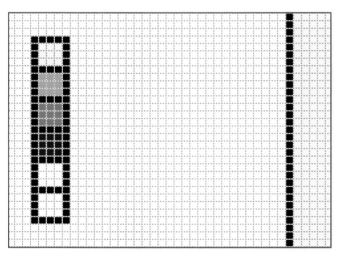

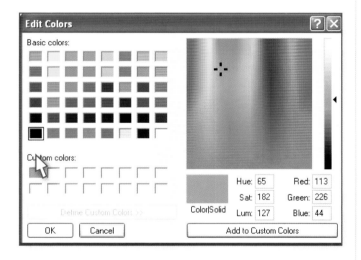

5 You can add new colors using the process described in steps two and three, but if you'd like to use a shade of the previous color, click on it in the Custom colors area.

6 To adjust the shade, use the slider on the right side of the dialog to select a lighter or darker shade of color, then click *Add to Custom Colors*. The next Custom color box will change to show your new custom color. Then click *OK* to return to the main window, where your color will appear in the Color box. Repeat these procedures until all your colors are chosen.

7 When you save your design and switch off the computer, Paint does not retain the changed color palette; so before you close down the program, make a color key at the side of the design with all of your chosen colors, even if you have not yet used them on the pattern. Select the color black and use the Line tool (\ ) to draw the key, as described on pages 20-25.

8 Select the Fill With Color tool ( ), then click on one of your custom colors in the Color box. The color will be selected (appearing as the foreground color in the bottom left of the screen). Now click in a square of the key you drew to fill it with that color. Click on another color and a different square and repeat until all your custom colors have a square in the key.

Patchwork Projects

2

Rainbow Squares

This is a bright wall-hanging using scraps of leftover fabric. I made each square on the grid represent one and a half inches, so, allowing a ¼-inch seam allowance, it only required 2-inch squares of fabric for the whole squares. To simplify making the half-square triangles I used the method outlined on page 23. Once you have your half-square triangles, trim them to the exact size needed.

Using the CD Templates

As an alternative to drawing the grid, you can use the *P30-Rainbow Squares.bmp* from the CD's *Templates* folder.

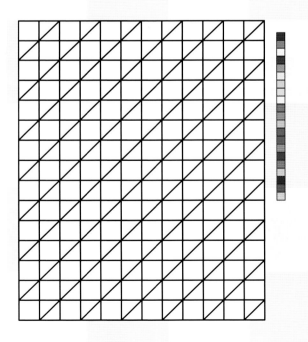

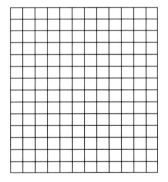

1 First decide how many squares you want to use. The illustration has 12 squares horizontally and 14 vertically. The design can be any number of squares and the size of the final stitched squares can be any dimension you wish. Draw a basic 4 × 4 grid of 12 pixels or open the 4 × 4 × 12 basic grid from the CD, then use *Select > Edit > **Copy*** then ***Paste*** to extend this to your required size.

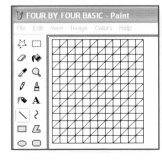

2 Once the grid is complete, using the Line tool (\) and the color black, draw diagonals across every alternate square to form the design template.

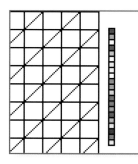

3 This now needs coloring, and the rainbow design is a good exercise in customizing colors. I created a color key next to the design three shades of each of the seven shades of the rainbow: blue, green, yellow, orange, red, violet, and indigo. Creating the colors and shades is described on page 26.

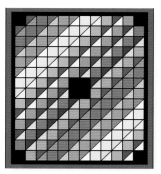

6 Experiment as much as you like, before choosing your favorite variation; I chose to add dark fabric at the center and corners, and add a border. The whole squares in the design are mid-tones, with triangles of light and dark tones to either side.

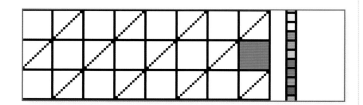

4 To add any of your colors to the grid, select the Fill With Color tool (⬧), then immediately afterwards choose the Pick Color tool (✐). Click once on your chosen color from the key and two things happen: that becomes the selected color and the Fill With Color tool (⬧) is re-selected. Now all you need to do is click in a square to apply the color, and use the Pick Color tool (✐) to change colors whenever you need to.

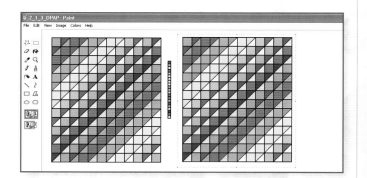

5 Complete the basic rainbow pattern using the method in step 4, before saving your basic design using *File* > **Save**. Using the Select tool (⬚), highlight the pattern and click *Select* > **Copy**, then *Select* > **Paste**. Click and drag the copied pattern elsewhere on the page. This gives you an additional pattern to experiment with (see page 18 for more on copying).

Stitched version
I pre-sorted all my fabric scraps to match the light, medium, and dark tones of each color, then chose at random from the correct pile.

Courthouse Square

The basis of this design is a simple grid at a 45° angle, like so many tiled floors. I chose a multi-colored floral design for the centers, picking up the purple, pink, and green for the pattern. I tried replacing the green with cream, but decided to stick with the original. This design is built using an "on point" (diagonal) basic grid.

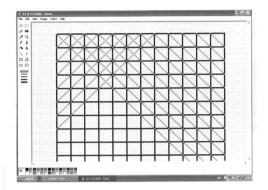

CD Files

If you want to work from step one with a basic 12 × 12 × 9 grid, open the file *Grids > Basic12x12x9*. If you'd like to skip to step 4 (the complete diagonal grid), open the file *Templates > P32-CourthouseSquare*.

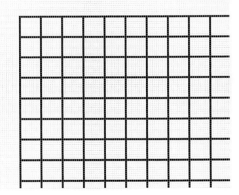

1 Create or open a saved basic 12×12×9 square grid or use an accurate six inch grid in 0.5 intervals. Click *View > Zoom > Custom* and choose at least 600% to obtain a workable size (see page 19 for more on zooming and grids).

2 Select the Line tool (\) tool and a color other than black—I'd suggest a shade of gray. Draw the diagonal lines by clicking at one end of the line you want to draw, then again at the other (*see page 23*). Continue until the whole diagonal grid is complete, including the outside edge. Be sure to use a transparent background.

3 The black lines need to be erased. Use the Fill With Color tool (◈), select white from the color box, then point the cursor over the line to be cleared and left-click. The line will be deleted.

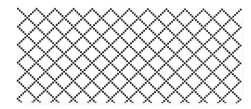

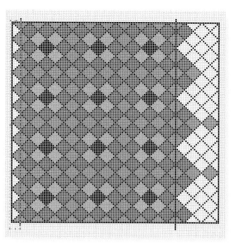

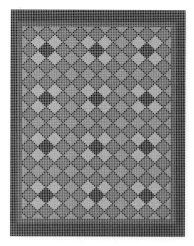

4 When the excess lines have all been cleared, select black and, using the Line tool (\), draw over the guide lines you created in black. You now have a basic grid for "on-point" designs. Save this with your basic grids to be used whenever needed. If you need a larger working grid, use the copy and paste method (*see page 18*) to add to the original.

6 If you wish to trim the overall size of your pattern, choose black and use the Line tool (\) to define the required boundaries. Then switch to the Select tool (⬚) and highlight the area you no longer require. Be sure to mark right up to the edge of your design, then click *Edit > **Clear***.

7 If your new edges from Step 6 stick out too far, use the Eraser tool (⬚) to tidy them up. Finally, add borders using the Rectangle tool (⬚) (*see page 42*) and color them as you like until the design is complete.

5 If you have already chosen your fabrics, customize your color palette (*see page 26*) to reflect them. With that accomplished, fill the squares of the grid using the Fill With Color tool (⬚). (Simply click on a color in the color box to select it, then click inside a square to apply that color.)

Finished quilt
Using two-inch squares (excluding the seam allowance) with a ¾-inch and 2-inch border, the completed quilt measures 34 × 42 inches.

Seven-Patch Bear's Paw Quilt

The Bear's Paw block remains one of the most popular designs, even though it has been used for more than a century. The block consists of four pawprints with pads and claws, set in sashing with a center square. Traditionally the pads, claws, and center square were in the same color, but with the variety of fabrics available today, many color combinations are found. Changing the single pad to a four- or nine-patch pieced square gives even greater flexibility. An entire quilt could be made using different pads for each block. Single paws also make a lovely border.

Using the CD Templates

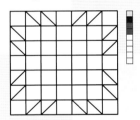

As an alternative to drawing the grid, you can use either the pre-drawn grid from the CD, which completes step one (*Grids > 7x7x18*) or the template file (*Templates > p34-BearsPaw*) which takes you as far as step 3.

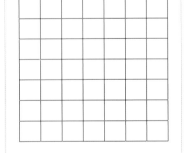

1 First you will need to acquire a 7 × 7 basic grid. If you do not have a program that produces this, follow the instructions on pages 14–16 to create one, or open the 7 × 7 × 18 grid from the CD. Each side of each square of this seven-patch grid contains 18 pixels so that it is clear for you to see.

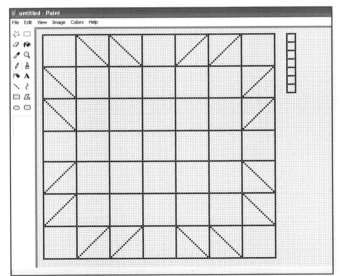

2 This then needs to be subdivided into one Bear's Paw pattern. Follow the plan, adding the diagonal lines using the Line tool (\). Place the cursor on one end of the line to be drawn, left-click and drag to the other end of the line, then release. Right-click to delete. Use *View > **Zoom*** whenever necessary to enlarge the work to make it clearer to see.

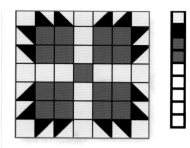

Edit Colors

Basic colors:

Custom colors:

Define Custom Colors

OK   Cancel   Add to Custom Colors

Color|Solid

Hue: 134   Red: 171
Sat: 220   Green: 223
Lum: 199   Blue: 252

3 The 7 × 7 block now needs to be colored, either using colors shown in the Color box or by customizing colors following the procedure detailed on page 40, including the color key. It is useful to create the color key as it can also be copied and pasted into other documents.

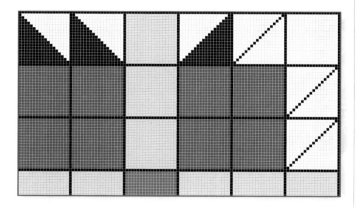

4 Using the Pick Color tool (✏), point and left-click on the chosen color. Then, using the Fill With Color tool (🎨), point and left-click on the area to be colored. If you make a mistake, simply choose another color and apply that instead, or alternatively the last three moves can be erased by clicking *Edit > **Undo*** or pressing Ctrl+Z.

5 When one block is complete, select it with the Select tool (⬚) then click *Edit > **Copy***, then *Edit > **Paste*** to build up your quilt design. If your page size needs to be increased, use *Image > **Attributes***, then increase the width or height. This can be done at any time.

It is easy to use the copy and paste method to experiment with color changes and arrangements and make sure that your final design is exactly the one of your choice.

Possible bear's paw variation

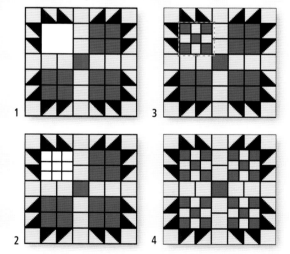

One posssible variation on the pattern is to create smaller patches inside the bear's paw design.

1 To replace a paw with a four- or nine-pieced design, first delete the paw by highlighting it with the Select tool (⬚), then clicking *Select > Delete*.

2 Use the Line tool (\ ) and black to draw in new gridlines in the paw space.

3 Color this, just as in step four, using the Fill With Color tool (🎨).

4 Use the *Select* tool (⬚) to highlight the new 3 × 3 area, then copy and paste it, just as in step five, wherever you want it to replace the original.

6 Once you are happy with your design or designs, it is time to plan the whole quilt. Use the copy and paste method to copy a number of complete blocks onto the screen, then use the Select tool (⬚) and drag them to try different arrangements.

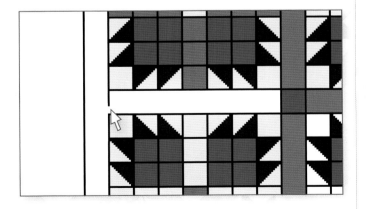

7 Experiment with different widths of sashing and types of border. Remember to complete each unit by closing off each area with the Line tool (\) before you fill it. Otherwise, when you click with the Fill With Color tool (🖌️), the whole screen color will be changed. (If this does happen by accident, the *Edit > **Undo*** or Ctrl+Z option will set it back to its previous state).

8 Complete your sashing by drawing lines all the way around the outside of your design before using the Fill With Color tool (🖌️) to apply your chosen color.

Finished article

I added 1¾-inch sashing and squares of the blue where the sashing lines met. I felt that the design needed a frame, but nothing to detract from the quilt pattern, so I gave it a plain 1½-inch border, then edged it with the bright blue.

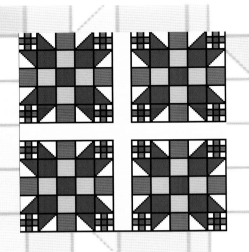

Sashing and Borders

Borders, like sashing, enlarge the quilt size, but whereas sashing frames individual blocks, borders frame the whole quilt. In the same way that a photograph or painting can be enhanced by a well-chosen frame, so a quilt can be made more complete by the addition of one or more suitable borders. However, it is not compulsory to have one at all. Sometimes the quilt design seems finished without one, while a busy pattern on another quilt may need a border to calm the effect. If the pattern seems to continue beyond the edges, even a small border will contain and complete the design. Borders are also useful for enlarging quilt sizes when necessary.

CD Files

The narrow border is applied to a 12 x 14 x 12 grid, which can be found in the grids folder under *Grids > 12x14x12*. The border design used on page 40 can be found in *Templates > P40-AddingBorders*.

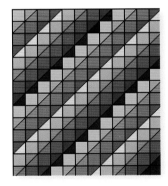

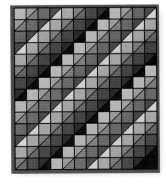

Even a very narrow border can finish off a quilt design.

Framing a centrally pieced block, like the Virginia Star, with several borders makes an effective feature wall-hanging. By selecting and copying plans of the quilt design on the computer and then adding borders, you have the opportunity to compare different styles and colors before a final one is chosen.

Planning a Border

There are three main styles of border – square, mitred, and ones with "cornerstones" or "junctions," where each corner has a design. Try each of these on your design copies to see which looks best.

Square corner top

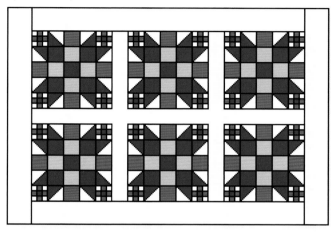

Cornerstones

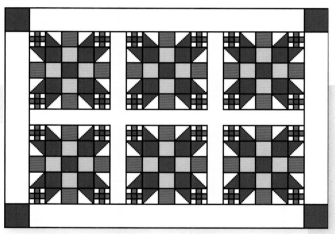

Hints on planning a border

There may seem to be a multitude of decisions to make, but spending a short time using the computer to view your choices takes a lot of the guesswork away. This means that the end result, after all the hours of hard work, should be one that you are happy with. It is surprising how changing just one element can create something very special, perhaps something that you had not thought would happen. Here are some ideas to try:

- A narrow, dark border next to the design frames it and draws the eye into an outer border.
- Think about repeating some of the shapes used in the quilt for the border.
- If the border of your choice doesn't turn corners easily, use a cornerstone.
- If a pieced border will not quite fit, adjust the depth of a plain border, or even add a plain border.

- If the border design is different at each corner, create a mirror image. Select half of the design using the Select tool, then click Image > Flip/Rotate to reverse the pattern.
- Select colors or even the same fabrics used in the quilt to give uniformity to the design.
- Continue the colors and design from the quilt into appliqué borders.

Drawing a border

The computer makes planning an accurate border, experimenting with colors, and numbering with the stitching order a simple task. Even small borders can be planned more easily using a computer.

Before

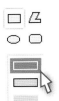

3 Now choose the Rectangle tool (▭) and choose the Outline Only option from the choices at the bottom of the Toolbar. Click on the last pixel of one of the lines you have created and move the mouse to the opposing one, releasing the button when you're there.

1 To add a plain border, you need to draw a box outside the edge of the design. Zoom into the top left corner and use the Line tool (\), or patiently (one-pixel-by-one-pixel) the Pencil tool (✏), to draw a diagonal line from the top right hand corner as far out as you want the border to be.

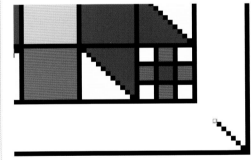

2 Repeat step one for the bottom right corner, this time making sure that your line is the same length as the first (for short lines, that's where the Pencil tool (✏) has its advantages).

4 Finally, remove the unwanted lines by switching to White and carefully clicking away the rogue pixels with the Pencil tool (✏).

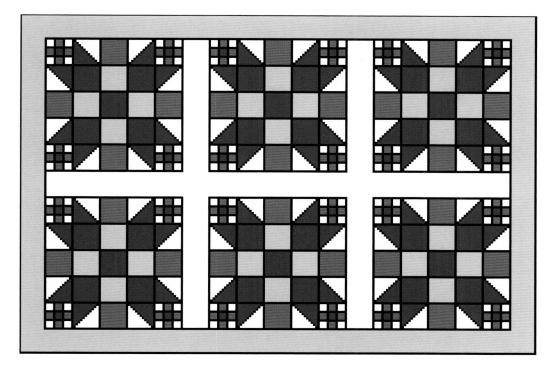

5 Select the color for the border, then use the Fill With Color tool (🖌) to fill the shape. If the border is too wide, use *Edit > **Undo*** and start again. If it is too narrow, draw another border outside this one and color it.

Additional features

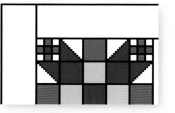

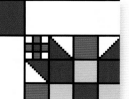

To add cornerstones, draw the box round the plan, then use the Line tool to extend the edges of the plan to the border line forming a square. Fill this in with either a different color or a pieced or appliquéd design. Use the copy and paste technique to fill each corner. Use the *Image > Flip/Rotate* command to turn the corner to face the right direction.

Represent mitred corners by drawing a line along the diagonal from each corner of the plan to the corner of the border. (If you miss out step four above, you're halfway there already.)

Planning the size of a pieced border is simple using the computer, as the border can be drawn and changed to fit alongside the design on the screen. *Select > Edit > Copy* then *Edit > Paste* small sections of a repetitive pattern to form the border, then select and drag to alter the positioning if necessary.

Designing a quilt using borders

Although there are certain designs that particularly suit being used in borders, any repetitive design can be adapted and used. For instance, several different stars could be repeated to make a star quilt, perhaps in a strippy design. A border could be composed from repeating a small part of the quilt design. It is your quilt to design as you wish. Using a grid on the computer will ensure that it fits together when you come to stitch it.

CD Files

You will find these desings in *Templates > P42-Borders*. The grid for step 2 can be found in *Grids > 14x14x12*.

Log cabin stitching

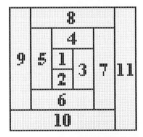

The log cabin is one of my favorite quilt designs. The numbers show the order in which it should be stitched.

1 First select some borders. Having looked at many borders, I picked out the ones I wanted to include in the quilt. You may prefer to change my choice for others, so I have included a selection of borders to give you some ideas. I particularly like Log Cabin so I had to include that. No border quilt would be complete without Flying Geese so that became the second. These are both quite busy designs, so I decided to have a simple pattern of squares to act as a counterbalance. I decided to use up scraps of yellow and blue from my scrap basket for parts of the design, as borders are usually composed of fairly small sections. As some of the scraps were too small to use more than once, the Square within a Square design seemed a sensible choice.

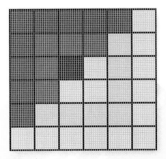

Log Cabin

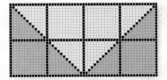

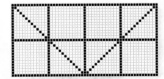

Flying Geese

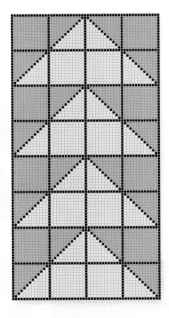

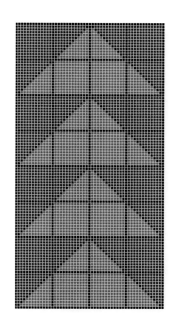

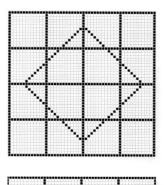

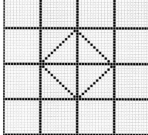

Square within a square

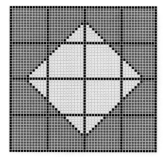

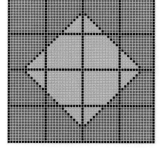

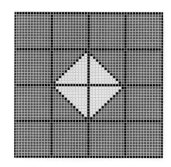

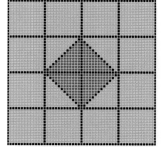

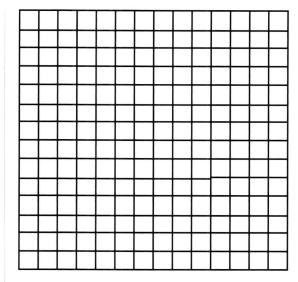

2 Acquire or create a basic grid of squares (*see page 22*). The grid used for this project was of 14 × 14 × 12 squares. I counted each grid square as one inch for the stitching. Be sure to use the same size grid for each border in the main quilt design, so they are simple to fit together later and make into a wall-hanging.

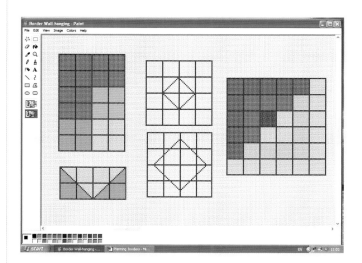

3 Start by drawing one piece of each border to be included (or which might be included). Each piece can be duplicated by first being selected, then copied and pasted (*see page 19*); use this method to begin to draw the border (leaving one square "stored" on an empty part of Paint's work area).

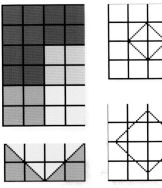

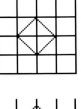

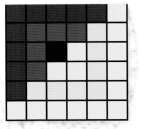

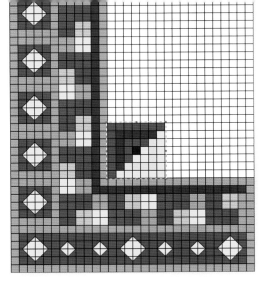

6 Try several options. For example, use the Fill With Color tool (🖌) to change lights for darks, or highlight your border with the Select tool (▭) and click *Image > **Flip/Rotate***. Use the Horizontal or Vertical options to create mirror-image shapes or to change the direction of arrow shapes.

4 Once a number of borders are ready, not necessarily colored, use the Select tool (▭) to highlight them, then click *Edit > **Copy*** and *Edit > **Paste***, dragging the duplicated borders around to see how they fit together. A plain strip of sashing is a good way to separate each border and make it clear. Without sashing, secondary patterns may become clear where borders join.

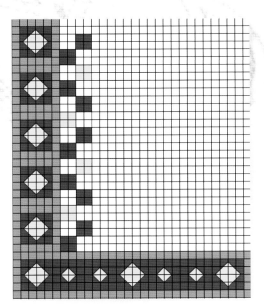

5 Originally, I used the border designs to create a strippy border pattern, but then decided to add corners and the final wall-hanging developed from there.

7 When the final design was almost complete, there was still one three-square strip left. I tried several designs to see which fitted best.

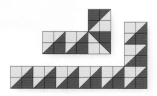
8 Finally I added blue sashing around the edges to finish off the design.

The finished quilt

Additional borders

Here are a selection of other borders that could easily be substituted for the ones in the wall-hanging, or be used to make the hanging into a larger quilt. They can be found on the CD in the *Borders* folder.

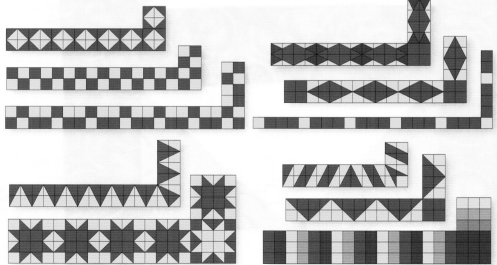

Basket Wall Hanging

All basket blocks comprise a number of half-square triangle pieces and have a base. The quilt used to demonstrate this is composed of eight basket variations and a quilted center. However, an extra basket pattern is included which could replace the center panel. The baskets can be used either square or "on-point," and both are demonstrated throughout the text. I find basket quilt designs quite irresistible, so had great fun with this one. Although I have designed a quilt composed of only baskets, a single block will add interest to a sampler quilt. I chose not to add a handle to any of these baskets, but instructions for adding one are given. When stitching the designs, look at the easy method for stitching half-square triangles given on page 11.

CD Files

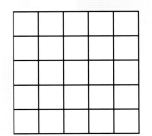

The blank grids for this project are the $5 \times 5 \times 19$ square for the square designs, or the $5 \times 5 \times 12$ for the "on-point" ones.

I had a five-inch charm pack of blacks, whites, and grays that were looking to be used in a quilt, so I added to these the purple-gray, two burgundies, a pink, and a green, then used a pale-green printed background and a black print. As there was only a small amount of each fabric, the blacks were used randomly, but shown simply on the computer as black, and where I wanted to select a specific square, these were depicted as gray. As the design is for personal use only, any method of color-coding can be used as long as you know the meaning.

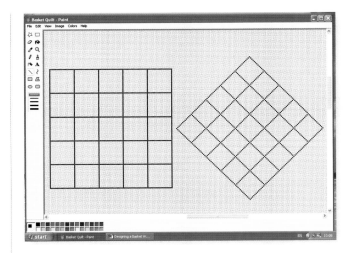

1 For each basket block you will need to create or open a grid for either a 5×5×19 square, or if you prefer, an on-point grid made from a 5×5×12 original (for more on this, use the method described on page 32).

Various basket designs

Here is a selection of designs, shown both as squares and as on-point designs. As you can see there is a surprising amount of variation possible from such a simple shape, and this is by no means the limit. The real purpose of showing you all of these is to inspire you to switch your computer on and create something new. Notice that there is no set line along the center between the basket and its contents as you might expect; the Fruit Basket allows its the top "fruit" patches to spill down onto the bottom (basket). Similarly the Broken Sugar Bowl adopts a different dividing line to the majority of the designs. Remember, there are no set rules, so create what you think looks good.

May Basket

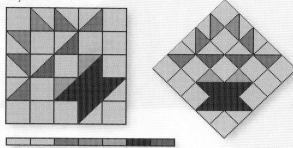

Anna's Basket

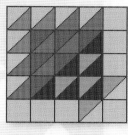 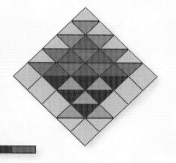

Fruit Basket

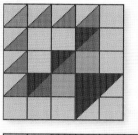 

Broken Sugar Bowl

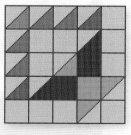 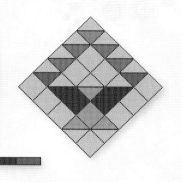

Mystery Basket

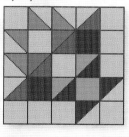 

Sugar Bowl of Cherries

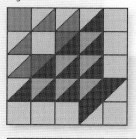 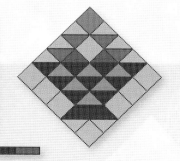

Basket of Diamonds

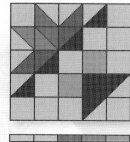

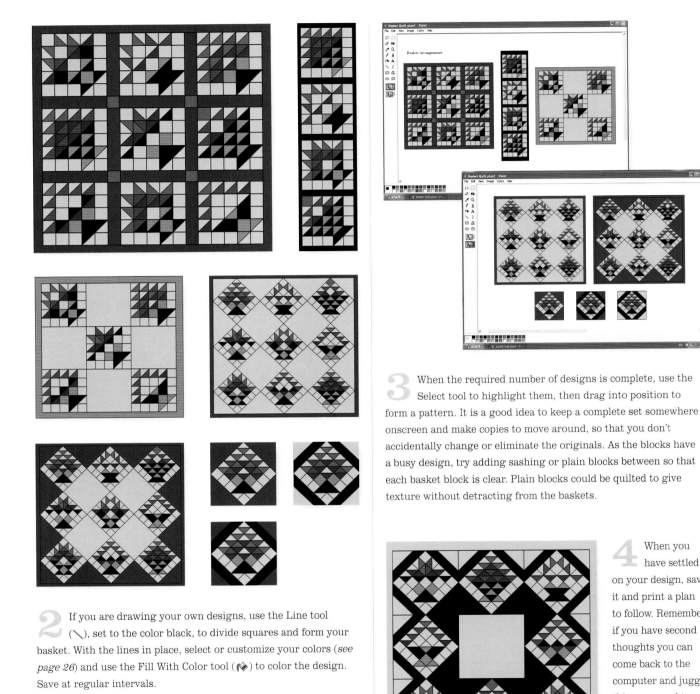

3 When the required number of designs is complete, use the Select tool to highlight them, then drag into position to form a pattern. It is a good idea to keep a complete set somewhere onscreen and make copies to move around, so that you don't accidentally change or eliminate the originals. As the blocks have a busy design, try adding sashing or plain blocks between so that each basket block is clear. Plain blocks could be quilted to give texture without detracting from the baskets.

2 If you are drawing your own designs, use the Line tool (\), set to the color black, to divide squares and form your basket. With the lines in place, select or customize your colors (*see page 26*) and use the Fill With Color tool (🖌) to color the design. Save at regular intervals.

4 When you have settled on your design, save it and print a plan to follow. Remember, if you have second thoughts you can come back to the computer and juggle things around to have a preview of how changes would look.

Adding a Handle

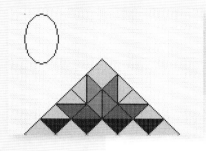

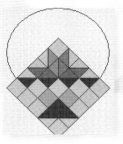

1 To form a basket handle on the design, which can be either quilted or appliquéd, you first need to take a copy of the basket plan that needs a handle using the copy and paste method (*see page 19*). Then, select red from the color box then, using the Pencil tool (✏), click on one pixel directly above the left-hand edge of the basket at the height where you want the top of the handle to be.

3 You will need to eliminate the excess ellipse pixels. To do this use the Pick Color tool (✎) and click on a neighboring pixel which is the correct color, then switch to the Pencil tool (✏) and click to repair that pixel. If you want the same handle on all the baskets on a quilt design, delete the excess squares from the first design, then use *Copy* and *Paste*.

A useful way to apply appliqué handles along the line of the pattern is to use fusible bias tape, which is available in different colors and comes pre-folded ready to iron in place and stitch.

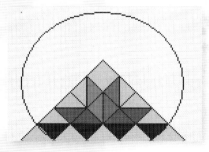

To create an accurate template for the line at the center of the handle, you will need to draw the basket plan on an accurate grid and create the handle on this.

2 Switch to the Ellipse tool (⬭), and be sure the "unfilled" option is selected. Place the cursor over the square and click with the right-button of the mouse. Drag it down and to the right until the edge of the circle touches the two top corners of the basket. Release the mouse. The ellipse will have continued down through the design.

4 Remember that adding a handle will increase the size of the block so the pattern will need to allow for this. Some ideas are shown for baskets with handles.

Quilted Basket Center

I decided to make the center of the hanging or lap-quilt a quilted pattern taken from one of the pieced designs. Handles could be added using the method described previously. A quilt could be made alternating pieced baskets and plain, quilted squares. Any of the pieced basket designs on the hanging could be adapted in the same way as this one to form the quilted squares. Embroidered or appliqué flowers could be added or handles outlined in the quilting. I used pearl and shell buttons with a few purple buttons which matched the quilt coloring to decorate the basket and a variegated black-and-white quilting thread for the quilting. To define the shapes further, use a quilting thread of contrasting color.

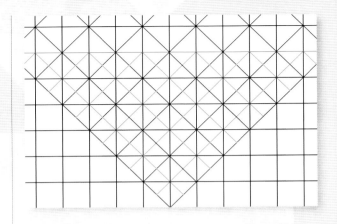

2 Draw a horizontal line across the center. In the area that represents the actual basket, below the center line, draw diagonal lines in between the originals to form small diamonds (shown here in red). When this is quilted it forms a checkered, woven pattern. Remember to save your work at each stage.

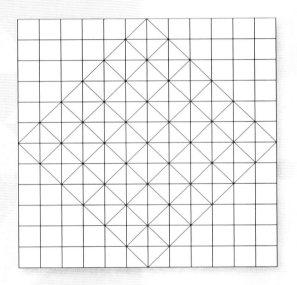

1 As the quilting needs to be a specific size to fit into the center square of the hanging, use an accurate grid. I used an accurate 6-inch grid in ½-inch intervals, counting each half-inch square as one inch. Printed at 200% this gives a 12-inch quilting pattern. Printed at 150% the pattern will be 9 inches. Use the Line tool (\) to form an "on-point" square onto the grid (this design will also use some of the original lines, so this is the best method).

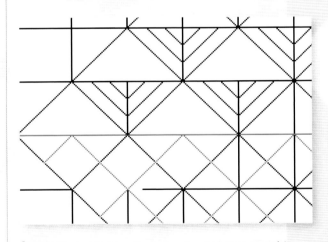

3 Use the Line tool (\) to add a simple pattern to alternate areas of the top half (use the basket designs from the previous page for inspiration). Leaving some areas unquilted helps to give a three-dimensional look to the finished design and make it more interesting. If more than one quilted square is being used, change this pattern on each one.

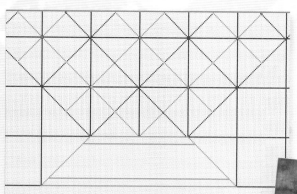

Centerpiece
Here is a detail of the design's center as it appeared when stitched.

4 Right-click on white in the Color Box to make white the background color. Now if you right-click with either the Line tool (✏) or the Pencil tool (✒), it will replace your chosen pixels with white. Use this technique to delete the excess horizontal and vertical lines leaving clear outlines to be used for the quilting pattern. Click with the left button and main color will be used; with this you can follow the diagram to create a base for the basket.

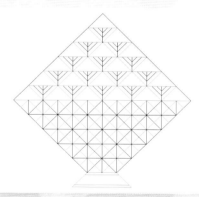

5 Finally, using the same technique as the last step, delete as many excess lines as you need to make the pattern clear for you to transfer to the fabric. On the diagram all of the excess has been deleted in order to make the final design clear.

The finished quilt
When complete, print the pattern to the required size, then transfer the design to the fabric using either a light-box tracing, pouncing, or by creating a tear-away stencil.

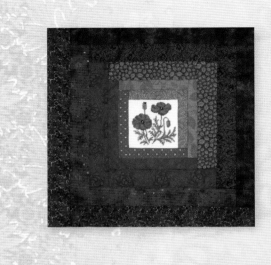

Log Cabin Quilt

The Log Cabin, a block which has been stitched in both England and America for two centuries, is one of my favorite designs. Traditionally it is stitched with a red center which has strips or "logs" along the edges, two sides having light colors and two dark. It represents the comforting inside of a house or log cabin. The red square is the fire which throws light on two sides, leaving the other two in shadow. However, the design looks good in many other color combinations too. The colors may also gradate from dark to light round the central square, either outwards or inwards.

CD Files

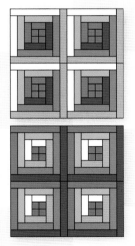

The blank grid for this project can be found at *Grids > 8x8x10*, while a colored version of the Log Cabin quilt block is in *Templates > BasicLogCabin*.

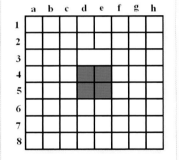

1. To construct one basic block using a grid, begin with an 8×8×10 grid. This basic pattern can be extended and continued to any size, but it is really when several blocks are put together that interesting tonal patterns develop. Choose a color then, using the Fill With Color tool (🖌), color the center four squares.

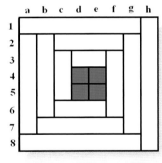

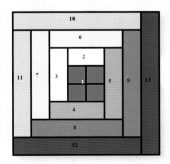

2. Use the Eraser tool (🖊) to delete the lines between some of the squares in order to end up with a design like the one illustrated. On your grid you will see the pattern emerging and can continue if you decide to use a larger Log Cabin block.

3. The block can now be colored following the procedure on page 26. You might find it helpful to fill in the sections of pattern following the numerical order shown; this is also the order for stitching each block, so it will become second nature.

Log Cabin Variations

From the basic pattern, many variations have developed and become blocks in their own right. Once you have constructed a basic block on the computer, any copies you make (using the Select tool (⬚) then Copy and Paste) can be flipped and dragged to form numerous different designs.

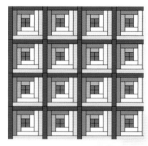 

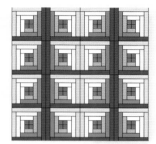 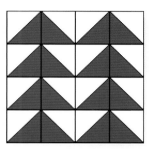

Sunshine and Shadow and Birds in Flight

A simple repetitive block like this blue and gray example, also called Sunshine and Shadow, is the basic Log Cabin design. This could also be a Birds in Flight design, because a Log Cabin block is similar in appearance to two half-square triangles, so it can be adapted to any designs using half-square triangles.

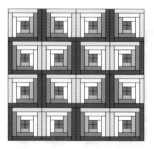 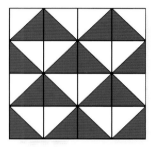

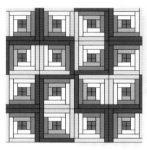 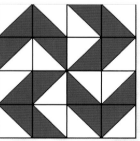

Wild Goose Chase

Wild Goose Chase and Wild Geese Flying would make a lovely wall-hanging with a plain border then a Flying Geese border. They show clearly how the Log Cabin block can give a new depth to a traditional design.

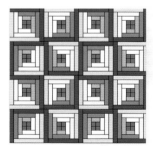 

Pinwheels

Both of these two designs are Pinwheels formed from Log Cabin blocks.

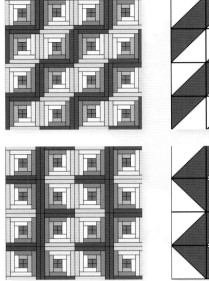 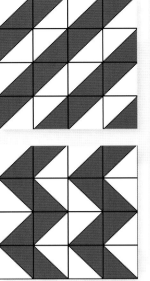

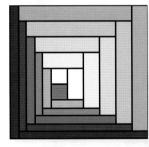 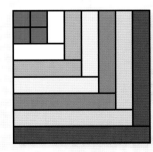

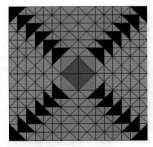

Straight Furrows and Streak o' Lightning

Rows, straight lines, and zig-zags of Log Cabin blocks all offer more ideas for using the blocks. Straight Furrows and Streak o' Lightning are particularly suitable for overall large bed quilts and can be extended easily to any size.

Medallion design

Log Cabin blocks are very effective for forming one large medallion design such as the Thistle. As these medallion designs are usually symmetrical, you only have to design one quarter or one half of the pattern, then select it and flip or rotate it using the Select tool (⌷) and the Image > Flip and Rotate option (as described on page 44).

Off Center

Full Off Center

Pineapple Block

Other variations

Other variations to try out on the computer before making a choice to stitch are to make the center square off-center to form a chevron pattern, or to vary the size of the "logs." The most complex traditional Log Cabin formation is probably the Pineapple block. This is a simplified version which shows how the structure can be formed.

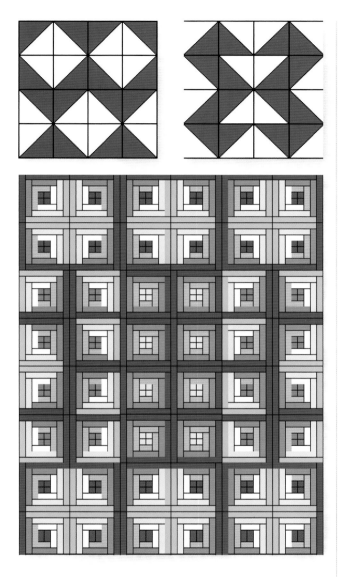

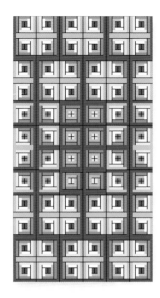

As the design grew too large to show on the screen, I reduced it to be able to view the whole quilt. To do this go to *Image > Stretch and Skew* (or press Crtl+W) then alter the *Stretch Horizontal* and *Stretch Vertical* figures (keep the values the same to keep the proportions). Press OK and the computer changes the design slightly to fit the required reduction, so the overall pattern can be seen. Always make sure that you have a copy of the full-size pattern before reducing or enlarging it. The example shows a reduction of 50% and 25%. Unlike a photocopier, the smaller the design becomes, the less detail is preserved (because the computer is trying to fit the same pattern onto fewer pixels).

Seahorses Quilt

As the blocks are the same size, try combining two or more patterns to make a quilt. This is shown in the Sea Storm and Sea Horses design. The patterns for the blocks are shown to the side. The top for Sea Storm, and the bottom for Sea Horses. It seemed appropriate to keep the sea theme and change the grays to greeny-blues by selecting the color and using the Fill With Color tool (🪣). I changed the coloring on the center blocks next to the seahorses in the same way.

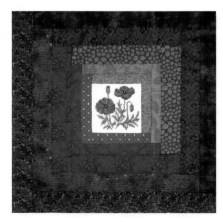

An example stitched Log Cabin block from the Poppy Log Cabin quilt on page 56.

The Poppy Quilt

Building on the principles of the Log Cabin design introduced on page 52, I decided to create a quilt made mainly from log cabin patches of different widths. The design forms a diagonal pattern by using similar colors for an adjoining two of the four sides of the log cabin design. These log labin patches effectively form a dramatic border for the central poppy designs.

CD Files

The Log Cabin design shown here can be found in *Templates > PoppyQuilt*.

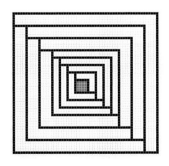

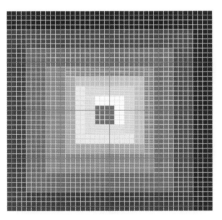

1 As I hadn't decided on the exact pattern and size of each block, I didn't use a repetitive basic grid, but worked out one block first, counting each row of pixels as ¼-inch, then copied this block to form the quilt. I started the pattern with a 1-inch square (¼ × 4 = 1, so the square was 4×4 pixels) in one of the darker reds. Then, following the same numbering as before, I added ½-inch logs by adding two pixels, then 1-inch logs which were four pixels, until I thought the square was big enough. This then became the block to be selected and copied.

2 As I had decided to use greens and reds to match the four cross-stitch designs which were to form the center of the corner blocks, I first customized a palette of colors. To do this, follow the process described on page 26.

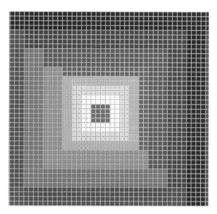

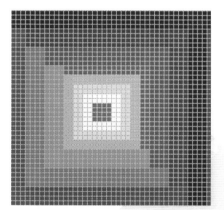

3 When one block is complete, save it either onto a CD or your hard drive, then highlight it with the Select tool and move it to the top of the screen to store it. While it's still selected, click *Edit* > **Copy** and *Edit* > **Paste** to duplicate it.

4 I wanted to include a 3-inch cross-stitch poppy design for the center of each corner block. To show a different center, like the cross-stitch centers to be used here, first select the center area, then click *Select* > **Delete** to clear it. I deleted a 16 × 16 pixel area to enable the 3-inch cross-stitch poppy to replace the "logs." Don't forget to add half an inch for seam allowances before cutting out. Move the completed square to the top of the screen to store with the first one.

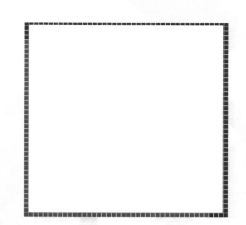

5 The third design to be included is the flower heads. Each of these would make a distinctive corner block. The block size must match the first block so that the blocks will fit together on your computer plan. Remember that this is a basic plan to allow a whole quilt to be designed. Although it is not accurate, it should be proportional, so take a copy of the first block and delete all the pixels inside it as you did in step 4, but this time leaving a border of just one pixel.

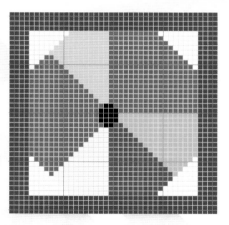

6 I gave my flower head a 1-inch (4 pixel) border. Draw the border within the block size in, then use the Line tool (\ ) to dissect the center horizontally, vertically, and diagonally. Mark points a quarter of the way along each edge (shown here in red).

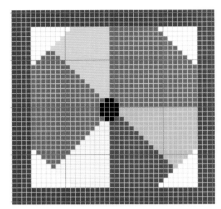

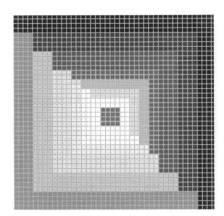

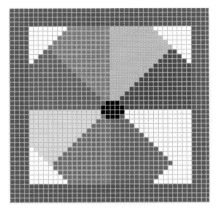

7 Join up the adjacent points around each corner to form the cut-off corners with the Line tool (╲), then delete the unwanted line pixels using the Eraser tool (⌀). Complete the block design using the Fill With Color tool (◈).

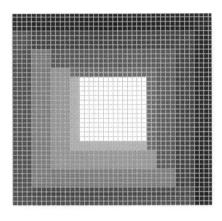

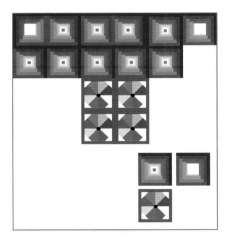

8 You now have three pattern blocks. Select and duplicate them, dragging the duplicates to form a design (see page 19 for more on Selecting, copying, and pasting). Keep the "master" copies on the screen as a reference and use copies of them to move around. Use *Image* > **Flip or Rotate** to create opposing versions of each block so the design can be symmetrical.

Undo

If you make a mistake, remember that you can use *Edit* > *Undo* or Ctrl+Z to go back by up to three steps. Using the computer means that you can see the complete quilt plan without even having used the rotary cutter. If you follow your plan, you only have to stitch the right combination of blocks and don't waste time or fabric.

9 Play around with your color choice. At this stage I decided to replace some of the greens with shades of cream. As individual pale creams are not clear on the computer, I used grays as a substitute. Working on a copy, I customized grays in the color box (*see page 26*) and used the Fill With Color tool (◈) to change the colors on this copy.

10 Print a color plan. Following this plan makes it easy to see the structure of each block. Without the plan this would have been quite confusing in this case. You can number the blocks on the printed plan and pin the corresponding number to the finished stitched block to make things even clearer if you wish. When working out the size of the strips, remember to add half an inch to cover the two ¼-inch seam allowances.

Final version

A design combining colored
shapes with log cabins.

Scrappy Herringbone Wall Hanging

The idea for this wall hanging originated in my having seen, a long time ago, a zig-zag design that I thought was called Herringbone. At the time I thought it would be a good design to stitch using up scraps of fabric. However, when I came to actually design and stitch it, I realized that it was probably the one-patch design called Chevron. As I have rearranged and changed the design, I am still calling it "Herringbone." Although it would be possible to machine-stitch the design using long strips of fabric, I intended to use up lots of scraps of different fabric, following the English method of stitching over paper templates.

CD Files

You require a 12-pixel basic grid. Open the file *Grids > 14x14x12* grid from the CD. The actual pattern size on the computer is 4 × 3, but working on a larger grid makes it easier to paste the shapes accurately in place. When making the quilt I used a 1 × 4-inch template and a 1½-inch square, but any size could be used. The CD file for step 4 is *Templates > Herringbone*.

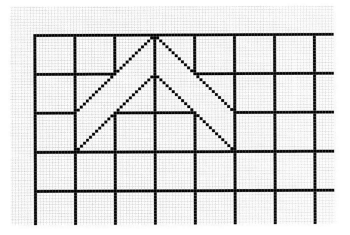

1 Using the Line tool (\\), copy the plan onto your grid, leaving the left-hand row of squares empty, as this can be copied to use for sashing or developing a square pattern later. If your secondary color is white, right-click with either the Line tool (\\) or the Pencil tool (✐) to delete the grid lines within the pattern shape, but leave the top vertical line in place.

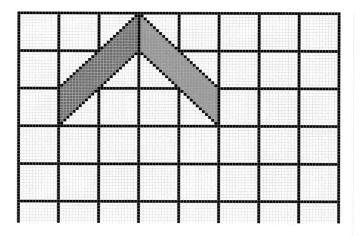

Use the Fill with Color tool (🖌) to color each side of the pattern in a different color. At this stage any two colors can be used.

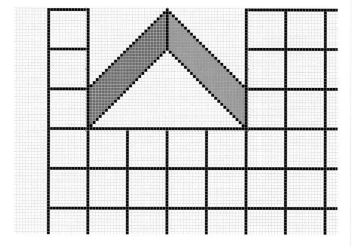

Switch to the Select tool (▦) and be sure that it is set to the opaque mode by clicking the option button at the bottom of the toolbox. Erase the unnecessary grid lines and select the whole chevron shape (the area highlighted here).

Use *Edit* > **Copy** then *Edit* > **Paste** to create a duplicate, position it beneath the original, then continue to do so until you have completed a whole vertical row. Now select the whole row, copy it and paste a duplicate adjacent to the original to form a complete pattern. By pasting more sections either vertically or horizontally, the pattern can be extended to any size.

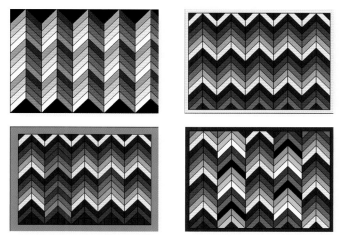

Colors can now be changed by choosing a color from the Color box or customizing a color following the Custom Colors procedure on page 26, then using the Fill with Color tool (🖌). Using lighter and darker colors or blocks of color can produce interesting effects. Use the copy and paste procedure to copy whole sections or rows wherever possible to save time.

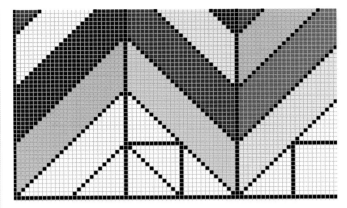

6 This asymmetrical variation was created by selecting one corner, duplicating and flipping it vertically, then highlighting the whole top half, duplicating and flipping horizontally. This could give the basis for a wonderful bed quilt, although it might be prudent to use larger templates.

8 To complete the edges where the chevrons finish, either fill the end in as one triangle, or continue the lines to form part-chevrons.

9 I decided to limit the range of colors in my wall hanging, and sorted out blues and beige/browns from my scrap-bag. Any piece that was at least $4\frac{1}{2} \times 1\frac{1}{2}$ inches was sorted into lights, mediums, and darks of blue and brown and then used randomly to match the tones of the pattern. I finally chose a design with three strips at each side and two in the center, with each section being separated by a square.

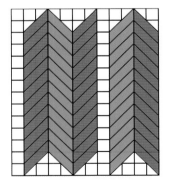

7 To add squares between some of the herringbone rows, select and drag the whole design to one side of the pattern, keeping in line with the grid but leaving a gap in the pattern. Now copy and paste the blank row of squares from one side of the pattern and select and, if necessary, move the other section of pattern back to close the gap. Coloring all of the squares in one color shows the effect of adding sashing to divide the rows. Varying the width of the sashing gives an interesting optical illusion of the lines not being straight.

Original choice for wall-hanging

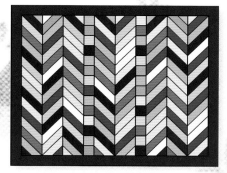

Comparison
Design with final
refinements in place.

On-point points
Try adding on-point squares at
the bottom of each chevron.
Using a 14 × 14 × 12 grid, copy
the same pattern, and follow the
same procedure as before to draw
and color it. It is similar to the
basic Herringbone, but each
diagonal line continues down to
make an on-point square.

Final Quilt
I resisted the temptation to
part-select the pieces and was
very pleased with the completed
hanging. I was quite sorry to
finish this quilt, but have plans
for a similar one in the future.

Star Wall Hanging

The star wall hanging includes several different techniques. This procedure will work for any multi-size blocks, so it may inspire you to resurrect all those hidden blocks and use them to create your own wall hanging. The computer acts as a design wall, and allows you to not only organize the blocks that you have already stitched, but also plan the blocks, strips, and borders needed to complete the project. It provides the opportunity to easily try colors, shapes, and sizes to make sure your hanging is balanced and interesting. It is a good idea to work out and save the plans for all of the blocks that you may want to use on one screen, so that everything is easily accessible.

Using the CD Templates

As an alternative to drawing the grid you can use the files *Grids > 7x4x8* and *Grids > 4x4x12*.

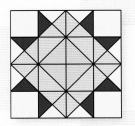

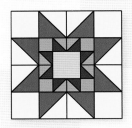

Alternatively, you can find blank star patterns in the folder *Templates > p64-Stars* called:
RisingStar.bmp
NoonStar.bmp
RoyalStar.bmp
ClaysChoice.bmp
HiddenStar.bmp
AirCastle.bmp
SquaresInASquare.bmp
Trees.bmp
Spool.bmp

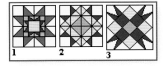

1 The first step is to choose some of the blocks that you may wish to include. These need to be planned on grids so that they can all be put together later. I decided to use three main stars as the most prominent blocks in the quilt, and to use seven other elements as well. These are looked at individually on pages 65-67, but should be added side by side, one after the other, like this.

2 Somewhere on your page you will need to create a color key, just as on page 26. This means that whenever the program is closed down but the file saved, you will still have an easy source of colors. Additionally, creating a single key before you create all your individual block designs will help you pick consistent colors. (Use the Pick Color tool (✏) and the Fill With Color tool (🎨), to take colors from the key to your designs, also as described on page 26.)

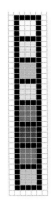

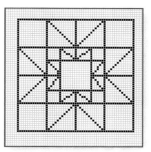

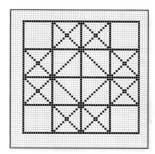

Rising Star and Noon Star

Both the Rising Star and the Noon Star need a 4 × 4 × 12 basic grid. Either create your own using the methods on page 22, or open one from the accompanying CD. You need to have a consistent unit of measurement so that the sizes of the blocks represent the stitched piece. I use one pixel to represent ¼-inch, so every square represents three inches.

Using the Line tool (\) and black, complete the pattern lines on the grids as shown in the diagram. You could substitute any other block of the same size. There are a number of star blocks on the CD.

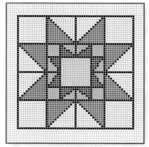

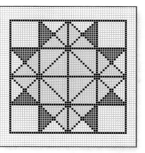

Complete the star designs using the colors of your choice. The quilt shown uses cream (background), green, two deep reds (one shown as burgundy, the other as a lighter red to distinguish between them), two tans, a brown fabric with large flowers, and a small-flowered beige-brown. If you have specific colors of fabric, customize the colors to the nearest match (see page 26); in either case, keep your color key updated as you do so, so you can use it for the other blocks.

Select then drag each completed block pattern to the top of the screen to store it. This leaves space below to work on the others. If the work-page needs to be enlarged, click on *Image* > *Attributes* and alter the width and height. The page may not appear to change, but it will have extended. Repeat this at any time.

Royal Star

This needs the grid squares to be "on-point." To follow this quilt design use the Line tool (\) set to black to draw one diagonal square with ten pixels on each side. Copy and paste this to form a nine-patch square, then complete the horizontal and vertical sides to form the full square.

Still using the Line tool (\) set to black, copy the lines (highlighted here in green) in each corner. Select and drag the color strip onto the screen and use the Pick color and Fill with Color tools to color the pattern. Select and drag it to the top store and save. This design will stitch up to be 12¾ inches.

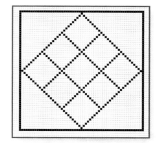

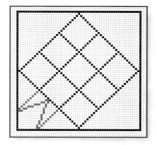

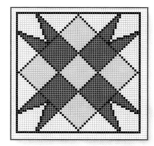

If you are creating your own design and need the basic grid to fit into a sampler quilt, for instance, start by drawing the outside edge of the whole block, then draw lines from the centers of each edge to create the on-point square and then draw the number of gridlines needed for the design.

As it is only a basic grid, primarily to allow you to see the overall effect of the quilt, it is more important that the outer edge fits correctly into the design than that the pattern is completely accurate in size.

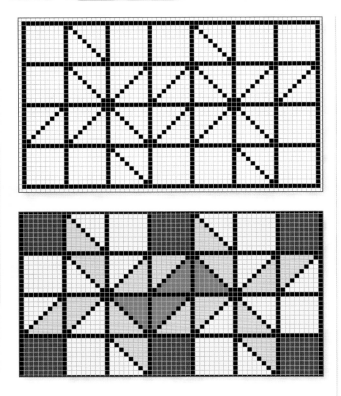

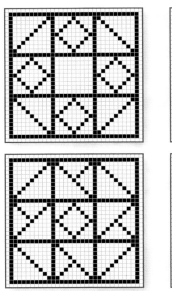

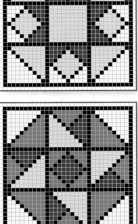

Variation of Clay's Choice

As this is quite a large design, I decided to stitch it with 2-inch squares. As four pixels represents one inch, each side of the squares needs to be eight pixels. You need to acquire a $7 \times 4 \times 8$ basic grid. Draw one square then copy and paste as before. Adjust the magnification using *View* > *Zoom* as needed. Choose black and the Line tool (＼) to complete the pattern lines on the grid, then color using the Fill With Color tool (🖌). As with the others, select and drag the completed design to the store at the top of the page and save when you are ready.

Hidden Star and Air Castle

These both need a 3×3 grid with 2-inch squares, which would be a $3 \times 3 \times 8$ basic grid, but they need to have an odd number of pixels, so either draw a $3 \times 3 \times 9$ basic grid or open the $3 \times 3 \times 9$ basic grid from the CD. This means that the pattern will be about ¾ of an inch larger than the stitching. You can see the variation between the pattern and my stitched quilt. When I stitched the design, I added a small border between the two designs. Follow the same procedure for drawing, coloring, and saving the designs as before.

Squares within a Square

These need a 4 × 4 grid, and I want the block to be six inches square, so each square will be one and a half inches, but once again they need an odd number of pixels so use a 4 × 4 × 7 basic grid. As before, the pattern is larger than the actual stitching, but by one inch this time. In other words, one pixel extra on four squares is four pixels extra, so that is ¼ × 4, or one inch. I have added a cream border at the bottom that links the Noon Star and Rising Star to take up the extra space. Complete these two as before.

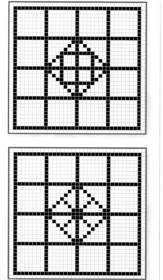

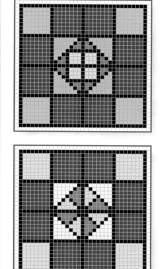

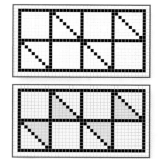

Spool variation

For this block a 4 × 2 × 8 grid is needed. This can be drawn or opened from the CD. It is a straightforward block to divide and color, following the diagram. This also makes a simple but effective border design.

Trees

These are foundation-pieced and are three inches square and will have a border. The patterns for these can be found on the CD. As the detail wouldn't show, use a background or plain green square with 12 pixels to represent the trees. Add a border, but this may need to be adjusted later. There are three trees on my final design, so I needed three squares for the plan.

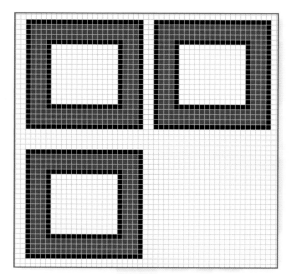

3 The main blocks for the Star quilt are now complete, and they can now be arranged to form different wall hangings. From left to right, the blocks shown are Rising Star, Noon Star, Royal Star, Variation of Clay's Choice, Hidden Star, Air Castle, Squares within a Square, Tree borders, and Spool Variation.

4 Use the computer as a design wall. Using the Select tool ( ), highlight any of the block designs from the top of the page, before copying them. Try to arrange the copies in the main area, picking out and working around any dominant grids.

5 Sorting out the arrangement is rather like putting together a jigsaw puzzle, and sorting the blocks that dominate either because of their shape, color, or size is like picking out the edge pieces. It gives you somewhere to start. If there are two similar blocks it may be better to separate them to balance the design. If you need to rotate one of the blocks, select it, copy it, and then click *Image > Flip and Rotate*. Don't worry if there are spaces between the blocks. These can be filled using sashing strips or pieced or appliqué borders. You may even decide to cut up one of the blocks and try it in a different way. As you have a master copy, this can soon be put right if it doesn't work out.

6 When you have settled on an arrangement, line up the outside edges and add sashing connecting strips or blocks until the hanging is complete. Using the Fill With Color tool ( ), try them in different colors to balance the overall arrangement. The blocks are to be used as a plan and are not accurate on screen, but they can easily be adjusted with the fillers when the stitching is being done. If you want an accurate plan, use the accurate grid, but the design will be too big to view as a whole. It is possible for each block to be drawn accurately, printed, then cut out to be arranged, but this would take longer. The black dividing lines that appear obvious in a basic grid almost disappear in an accurate print and would form the cutting-out lines.

Before connecting strips

After connecting strips

Stitched version

The quilt here has been finished with button detailing, carefully placed to accent the points of interest.

Designing a Hexagon Wall Hanging

Hexagons were one of the early patchwork shapes. The Victorians stitched variations of Grandmother's Flower Garden, using tiny templates and expensive fabrics. These patchworks were for decorative use, perhaps over furniture. They used the English pieced technique, hand-sewing over templates. Regular hexagons are common, with equal sides producing a honeycomb effect, but templates can be any size or shape. This includes the church window (elongating a hexagon along two sides), or the coffin shape. They combine well with squares, rectangles, and triangles.

CD Files

The basic hexagon shape can be found on the CD in *Templates > Hexagon*, as can a larger grid in *Grids > HexagonGrid*.

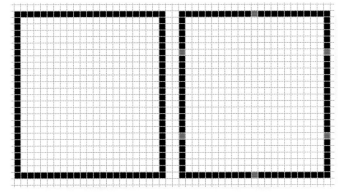

1 If you have a card, plastic, or metal template ready for your pieces, you need to measure it to create a proportionate grid. Measure your template from point to point and across from straight edge to straight edge, then multiply each measurement by eight. The wall-hanging template was three inches from point to point and two and a half inches from edge to edge. Multiplied by eight these measurements become 24 x 20.

2 Turning to Paint, as the shorter measurement of the rectangle must have an odd number of pixels in order to obtain the point of the hexagon, add one to the short side of the rectangle making this 21, and, in order to retain the correct proportions, add two to the long side, making this length 26. Zoom in to a large-sized screen with a grid, then, using the Line tool (\) set to black, create a box of these dimensions, i.e. 26 × 23. As shown, mark the middle of the short sides and a quarter of the way from each end along the long sides.

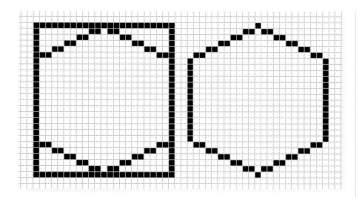

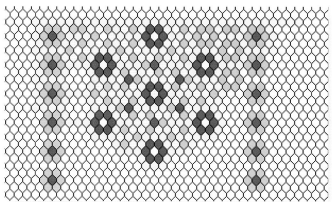

3 Now use the Line tool to join the marks to create a hexagon shape. With the right mouse button or the Eraser tool (⌀), delete the excess lines to leave the basic hexagon template in roughly the proportions to be used.

5 To color the hexagons, select or customize a color, then use the Fill With Color tool (🎨) (*see page 26*) to shade them. If you remember to click with the right mouse button on the color white, you can then use that button to delete an area of color at any time. There are a number of possible variations on the theme you might like to explore.

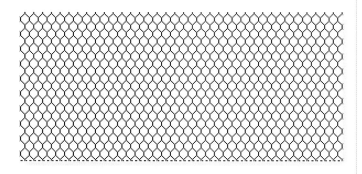

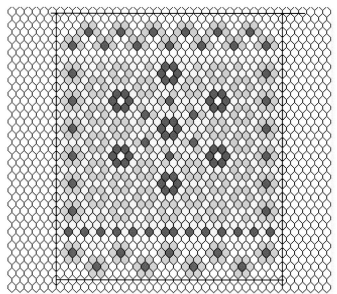

4 Save this, then use copy and paste (*see page 18*) and duplicate the original many times to form a large plan of hexagons. An accurate size doesn't matter as hexagons can be added or deleted at any time. Remember that it is possible to select, copy and paste a group of hexagons, which saves time and wrist energy! Complete the plan by drawing a line along the planned edge of the quilt design using the Line tool (╲), continue the pattern up to the edges, highlight the excess grid with the Select tool (⬚), and click *Select* > **Delete** to clear it.

6 Print a copy of the final design to use as a working plan, so that you can see exactly which hexagons are required. Having a plan to work from means that hexagons can be stitched together at any convenient time and that no unnecessary hexagons are cut or stitched.

Creating an isometric grid

A hexagon shape can be split into three diamonds to give a completely different set of designs. Tumbling Blocks or Baby Blocks is one of them. The grid needed for this design and several other diamond blocks is an isometric grid. This can be found on the CD, or you can create your own following the instructions. A basic square grid with an odd number of pixels is required. I used a 5 x 5 grid with 19 pixels between the lines.

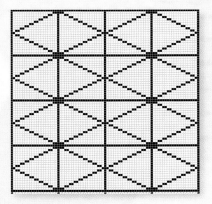

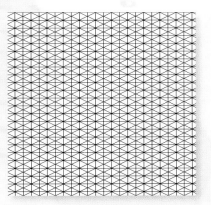

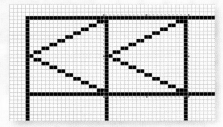

Using the Line tool ($\searrow$), work in the top-left square. Draw lines from the center of the left side to the top-right and bottom-right corners. Once you have done that, use the Select tool to highlight and click *Edit > Copy* to duplicate the square.

Now copy and paste both squares (the diamond shape) repeatedly to form an isometric grid. This can be extended at any time if your design requires more space.

Tumbling blocks

Using the isometric grid you can create a number of designs, like this "tumbling blocks" pattern with a three-dimensional look. Choose light, medium, and dark tones and fill in the grid, keeping the tones consistent in the same section of each hexagon. Use copy and paste to speed things up.

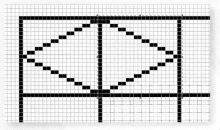

Click *Edit > Paste* to place a duplicate on the page, then choose *Image > Flip or Rotate > Flip Horizontal* to flip the lines. Drag the opposing square into place to complete the pattern.

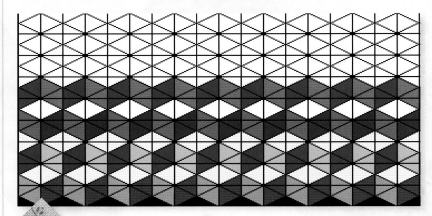

Using the same isometric grid, but extending the colored area, the pattern can easily be enlarged. Experiment with combining blocks of different sizes. Copy and paste a section of the grid to try out ideas, then select and drag the new sections into the main pattern. (Remember that *Edit > Undo* will undo up to the last three moves.) In this design the oversized blocks appear to be floating above the background.

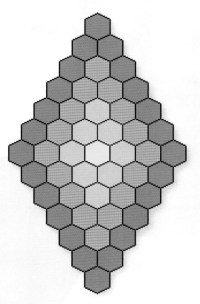

Grandmother's Flower Garden

Traditionally, the center would be yellow to represent the flower bud, the six surrounding hexagons represented the petals, and the next rounds were the grassy paths of the garden, so these would be green. Sometimes there would be extra rows of colored petals before the green grass. Often a diamond setting of the hexagons was stitched. The patterns show the double rosette and diamond designs.

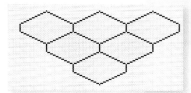

Coffin

If the angled sides are elongated, the shape is known as a Coffin. These shapes combine well with squares, rectangles, and triangles to form new blocks. Experimenting with these templates on the computer can produce some interesting effects.

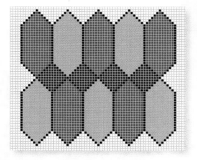

Church Window

When any two parallel sides of a hexagon are extended, it is known as a Church Window because of the resulting shape. This is shown on the tree design, which, if it were to be worked in fabric of strong, glowing colors, would resemble a gothic stained-glass window.

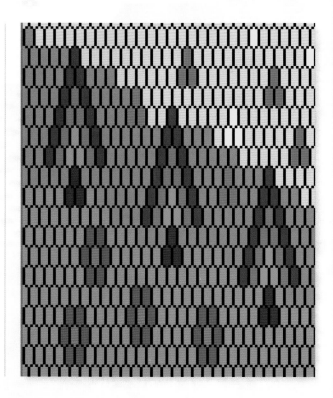

Alternative tree design

Save the design at intervals, and make copies on the same screen
to try different color combinations.

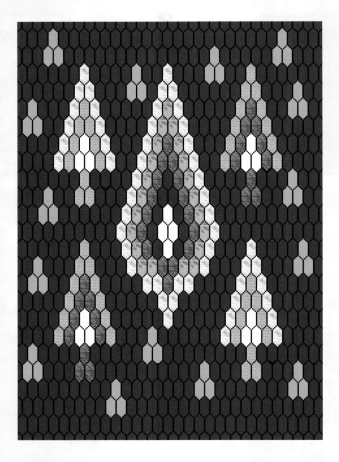

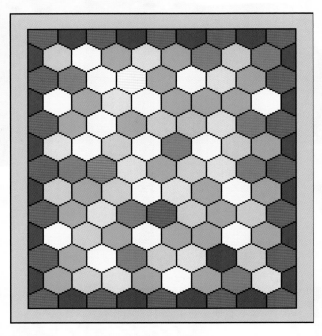

Wall-hanging design,

Although, traditionally, quilting is done in a hexagonal
design, I chose to add small beads to tie the design.

The design of the wall-hanging shown was not a definite pattern. I experimented with colors and fabrics on a grid of hexagons until I was happy with the design on the computer, then printed this as a plan. As I had a range of colors, some in limited supply, I used shades of color on the plan to represent a group of fabrics of the same tone rather than one color for each fabric. The actual fabric from the group was selected at random which meant that the final stitched design was more interestingly varied than the computer plan.

Baby Quilt or Playmat

This design forms a large multi-functional baby quilt that could be used initially as a padded mat to lie on, which is especially useful with wooden floors. It can then become a playmat and eventually a cover for a child's bed.

CD Files

For this design, work from a grid with squares of 33 pixels to each side (file *Grids > 3x3x33*), or if you change the size, you must use an odd number of pixels as it is necessary to have a center dividing line.

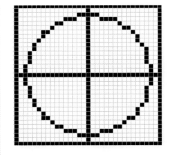

2 Using the Line tool (\), draw a horizontal and a vertical line to quarter the design. This has created your basic design grid for this pattern. To create an accurately sized pattern to use as a template, follow the same procedure using your accurate grid, but allow five clear pixels round the edge of the circle. Remember you have to add a seam allowance when cutting out.

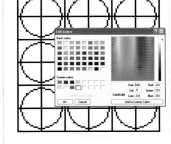

3 Copy and paste the number of blocks for the size of your project, as shown on page 19. If your screen doesn't show the whole pattern, use the scroll bars or a smaller magnification.

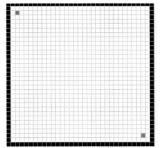

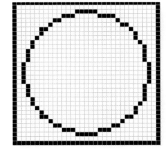

1 Working from a 33-pixel square as described in the box, click on the Ellipse tool (⬭), place the pointer toward (but not quite in) the top left of the square (as shown) and drag it diagonally to the blue square and release. You now have a circle in the center of your square.

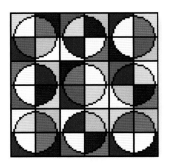

4 Switch off the grid (Ctrl+G), ready to color the pattern. On the examples, as there are eight sections to each pattern, I used four shades of pink and four shades of purple from a customized color strip (*see page 26*).

Possible variations

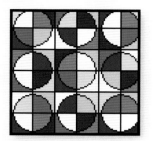

1 Random coloring

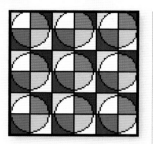

3 Repetitive coloring, dark and light border

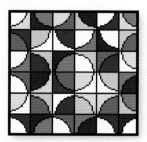

2 Use *Image > Flip* to form a scallop border

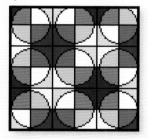

4 Variation of 3 using *Select > Image > Flip*

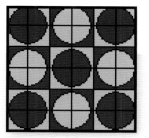

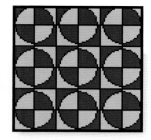

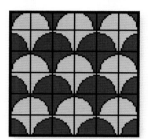

5, 6, 7, 8 Two-color plans. These can also be used as a scrappy quilt by dividing all the fabrics into darks and lights. The same overall impression will be obtained with random coloring. Number 8 actually forms a Shell or Clam pattern, of which 10 and 11 are variations.

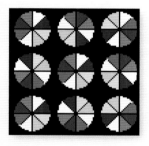

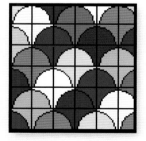

9 Diagonal lines have been added to divide the nine large squares into eight sections per circle. In this case I have used the same order of colors, but have rotated (*Select > Image > Rotate by angle*) the whole circle by 90°. This gives an overall balance of color.

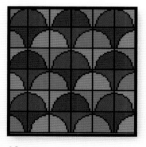

10 Shell or clam variation

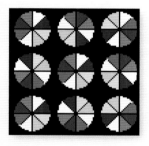

11 Shell or clam variation

Final design

Using a 5-inch square with a 4½-inch circle, the finished mat center measures 40 inches square. As I had limited amounts of some of the fabrics, I used alternating light and dark tones to create an even balance.

Foundation Piecing

The basic concept of foundation piecing is not difficult and enables small patchwork blocks to made quickly with a high degree of accuracy. Small points are made easy and lines miraculously meet at corners! Beginners and experts can create stunning results with a little care.

CD Files

The files for this page are in a folder called *Templates > Foundation*. They are called *TheSimpleLife*, *BlockPattern*, and *ChurchDesign*.

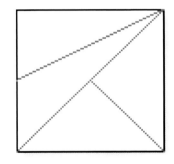

2 Plan

Foundation piecing enables the small points on the pinwheels to be stitched accurately. As the name suggests, a foundation of fine fabric or paper is used. This may be removed once the stitching is complete, or, in the case of fabric, may be left in to give stability. A pattern of lines is drawn, or printed using the computer, onto the foundation. Stitching is done either by hand or machine, along the lines in an organized numerical sequence.

The lines are drawn on the wrong side of the foundation. Fabric is pinned or placed on the right side and the stitching is done on the wrong side, following exactly the pattern lines. As it is stitched from the back, the patchwork becomes a mirror image of the original drawing. Using the computer for this technique has many advantages. As shown in the Seasons wall-hanging (*see page 80*), a pattern can be developed from a simple picture. Once this is done, the viability of stitching the design can be tested. If there is any doubt, then the pattern pieces can be numbered, using different colors for each section.

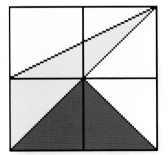

1 Picture

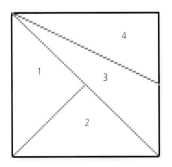

3 Plan flipped and numbered

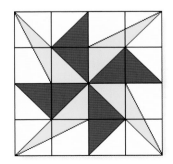

4 A final block pattern

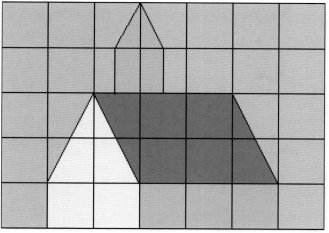

The foundation plan for a church design.

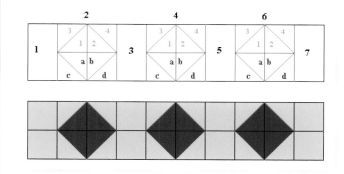

Reversed and numbered, ready to be stitched.

To overcome the mirror-image problem, the design can be selected and flipped in a few seconds. A colored plan will show the color reversal when it is flipped.

The plan can be printed to any size (*see page 24*) and multiple identical copies made, and more in the future from the CD or hard drive on which it has been saved. Using a photocopier or scanner can produce minor errors in size, which in a miniature quilt may be compounded to cause problems. As with printers, all copiers vary slightly, so all copies should be from the same source. Copies from copies should not be used for the same reason. Printing directly from the computer will eliminate this problem.

The computer allows the patterns to be arranged in various designs with different color combinations to plan the final quilt. Only the relevant blocks need to be stitched, thus saving fabric and time.

Number order

The computer makes planning an accurate border, experimenting with colours and numbering with the stitching order a simple task. Foundation piecing a border will enable a very precise border to be produced, a key factor in a small quilt. Unlike fabric, foundation paper doesn't stretch, so the border is not likely to be pulled out of shape or alignment.

The simple life

Even small borders can be planned more easily using a computer.

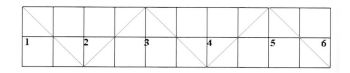

Foundation Pieced Seasons Hanging

When using foundation piecing, the first thing to consider is the design. Planning a pattern using a squared grid gives the accuracy needed for foundation piecing, but it is basically a straight-line pattern. I usually prefer to design initially using a basic grid and then transfer the final design to an accurate grid. This means that a whole quilt plan is visible on the screen to be worked on without having to scroll to see the hidden parts, and different options can be seen alongside each other. However, with a single small design it is possible to work directly on an accurate grid. To demonstrate the procedure to obtain a foundation pattern from a basic picture I have used a simple house and tree.

CD Files

This design was drawn on two grids, *Grids > 6x6x19* and *Grids > 8x7x19*. The template is called *Templates > Seasons*.

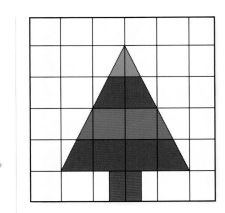

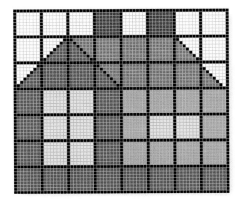

1 For both the tree and the house elements of the final design, acquire a grid, then use the Line tool (╲) to draw simple pattern lines, and the Fill With Color tool (◑) to color the design (just as in the examples earlier in the book).

Nothing is ever wasted

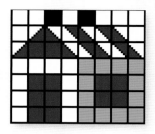

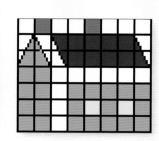

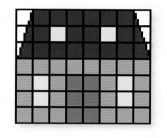

Originally, the plan for this wall-hanging had a different house for each season and there was to be a flower for spring and summer and a tree for fall and winter, so these were planned on the same worksheet. The final hanging only used some of the small patterns, but the rest are saved for another time.

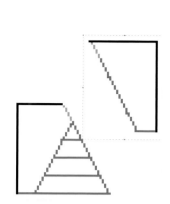

3 Don't worry about excess lines on the copy. Try to paste the copy pieces to roughly form the design shape so that it doesn't become a jigsaw puzzle. Right-click on the Line tool (\ ) to delete excess grid lines, leaving the pattern areas clearly visible. Save the file, then use the Select tool (⬚) to highlight each piece and drag back to re-form the design. Use this method to decide an order that you intend to stitch them (go back to the last save to try a new method).

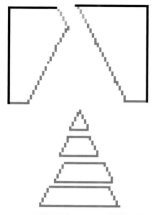

2 Remember that to make a pattern work, the design must be able to be stitched in a sequence of straight lines. It often helps to continue a line to the edge of the block, and you will need to experiment to find the approach you prefer—two alternatives are shown here in green. I chose to extend the line to the border to enable the background to be stitched in just two sections. The alternative would be to add the top row as a separate piece, creating a long seam line and making the piece more bulky.

Experimenting with gridlines

Copy and paste (*see page 19*) to make several copies that you can use to try different subdivision stitching lines. Choose a different color to the gridlines so that the sections are clearly visible. To check that the stitching will work, first make sure that the transparent background is selected. Use *Select > Edit > Copy* then *Edit > Paste* to make a copy of each section of the design.

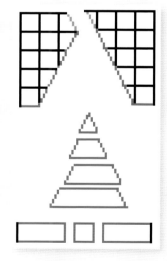

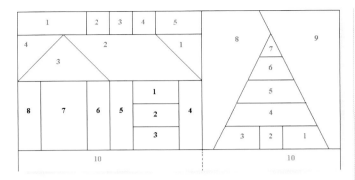

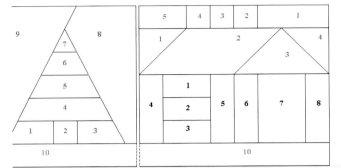

When the order is worked out, dependent on the difficulty, it may be useful at this stage to use the Text tool to add some numbering or lettering to the plan. To do this, Paint needs to be on Normal View. The basic plan becomes small, so add the numbers next to the piece rather than try to fit them inside. It is useful to color the text in each section of the pattern in a different color. For further information, see page 26. (An alternative is to print your ideas and cut them up, then actually lay the pieces on a board in order and write on the numbering or lettering.)

Remember that foundation piecing uses a reverse image of the picture. Use *Select > Image > **Flip or Rotate*** then choose *Flip horizontal* to reverse the pattern before adding the text so that it will be the right way round when you are working. Save the design again, so that copies are made showing both the way it will appear when stitched and the reversed pattern for printing. (The colors can then be removed by right-clicking while the Fill With Color tool (🖌) is selected and the right click (or background) color is set to white (*see page 26*).)

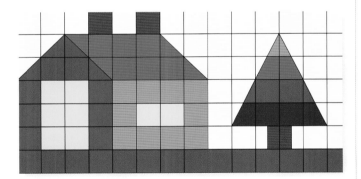

The plan now needs to be copied onto an accurate grid. Use part of your accurate 6-inch grid in ½-inch intervals. This can easily be printed at 200% to reproduce as inches, 400% as 2 inches and so on, but allows the pattern to be visible on the screen.

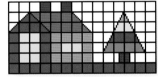 

 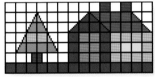

If you are using a paper base, cut the paper to fit in your printer and print the number of patterns that you need directly on to the paper. If you are using a foundation fabric, print onto white paper and use this as a stencil to draw over. The saved patterns can be used again in the future.

Final Design

The final quilt combines four variations of the same design, colored differently to represent the four seasons.

Countryside Quilt

This wall hanging illustrates how to use the computer to design a quilt using blocks of different sizes and using a variety of techniques. It includes foundation piecing, curves and appliqué, and both English and American techniques. First I took blocks with a countryside name or shape, then, using a limited selection of colors, worked out the individual blocks and put them together to form the design. It seemed appropriate to add small wooden buttons and shapes to give added interest, and I quilted following the curved lines on the curved flower, and the direction of the points on the compass design. Two reds, three yellows, orange, two greens, a floral fall print, a small floral for the center of the Honeybee, and three beiges were used for the quilt shown here. The quilt would make a cheerful addition to any room.

CD Files

These quilts are made using these grid files: *Grids > 8x8x19*, *Grids > 9x9x19*, and *Grids > 10x10x19*.

The countryside quilt is formed of one quarter of a Mariner's Compass (the sun). There are two flower blocks, two Sheepfold blocks, Leaves, Hen and Her Chicks, Honeybee, and Crow's Nest. An easy alternative to the foundation flower block is the pieced Blossomtime block, using an eight grid square for which I have included the pattern both in this section and on the CD. A pieced leaf with a small border could also replace the foundation-pieced one. As the individual blocks need to be arranged together, the same-size basic grid

needs to be used throughout the design. I used a square with 19 pixels inside the black outlines. An accurate grid would be far too big to see a whole quilt design on screen at any one time, so use a small "basic" grid. For the Mariner's Compass, for example, I used $10 \times 10 \times 19$ basic grid. These are for one quarter of a compass, which is all that is needed for this quilt design. Since it is such a dominant part of the design, I also used the $10 \times 10 \times 19$ basic grid for the whole-quilt design.

Mariner's Compass

Following the same procedure as the structure of this Mariner's Compass, it is easy to develop an individual compass design of any size with any number of points. It is pieced using the English method, so when the foundation plan is printed, a card template needs to be cut accurately for each segment, then covered with fabric. The segments are stitched together and the card removed. If your printer will print onto card, the pattern can be printed directly onto the card ready to be cut out. Print two copies, one to use as a master plan and one to cut up, then you have the plan to refer to without coming back to the computer each time. Otherwise having lots of cut pieces and no plan to match them to can be like a jigsaw puzzle.

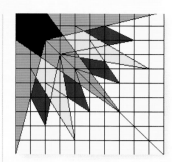

3 Customize your colors (*see page 26*) and use the Fill With Color tool () to color the design and make a color strip. Select and drag the colored design to the top of the worksheet to store. Save.

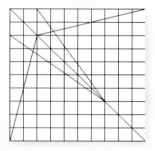 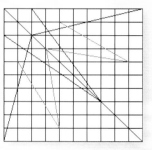

1 On the basic grid, using black and the Line tool (\), draw a diagonal to place the longest point of the compass, and draw the lines from the end of the point to the center as shown. Continue drawing the long points (shown in blue here to distinguish them). Notice that edges of the two adjacent quarters meet to form a point.

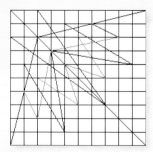 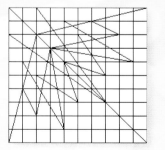

2 Draw in the intermediate points until the full quarter is complete.

4 One quarter only is needed for this Countryside Quilt design. To create a complete compass, select the corner then copy and paste it. Use *Image > Flip Horizontal* to mirror the quarter before moving it into place next to the original. Finally repeat this step with both quarters (and *Image > Flip Vertical*) for the second half.

Honeybee

In this traditional block, the shapes that are yellow in this design represent the bees and the center represents the flowers. I added a bee and four tiny black buttons to the finished block. This is a pieced block with appliqué added to the completed block. Creating a template for the appliqué will need an accurate grid, but to be able to see the whole quilt design you need to acquire a basic 8 × 8 × 19 grid (you can find this on the CD).

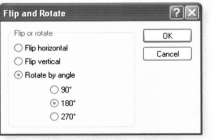

1 First, follow the plan for the colored block.

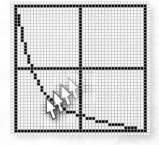

3 Place the cursor on the center of the diagonal and drag it towards the bottom-left corner of the square to form a curve. (Remember, *Edit > Undo* will let you have as many attempts as you like!)

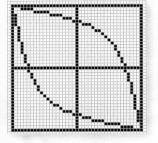

5 Make sure that you have a transparent background by clicking the box at the base of the toolbox so that the original curve isn't deleted, then select and drag one grid over the other to form the elliptical "bee" shape. Save this.

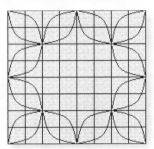

6 Copy and paste this shape onto the pieced block design following the plan. Use the copy, paste, and rotate method described under Mariner's Compass to create the full design.

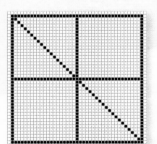

2 To form the "bees," take a basic 2 x 2 grid. Referring to the diagrams and using the Curved Line tool (⌇) and black, draw the diagonal line from top left to bottom right.

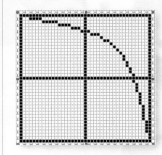

4 When you have created a suitable curve, copy and paste it then click *Image > Flip or Rotate* and choose *Rotate by angle* set to 180° to form the second part of the "bee" design.

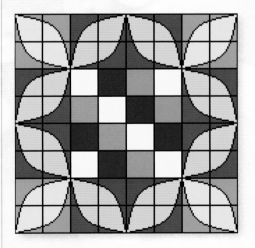

7 Save the design, color it, then select and drag it to the top of the page to store it before making the final quilt.

Curved Flower

Once you have mastered the basis of this block, you will be able to use it to devise countless curved designs of your own. It is primarily a curve within a square that can be used either convex or concave. The CD accompanying the book has several other alternative curved flowers (In the *Templates > p84-Countryside* folder).

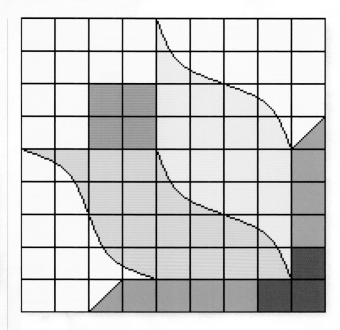

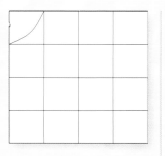 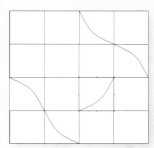

To fit the quilt design, each square needs to be 2 inches and one extra square is needed at the right hand side and bottom, for the leaves. So, use a $9 \times 9 \times 19$ basic grid, or a $4\frac{1}{2} \times 4\frac{1}{2}$ inch accurate grid, in $\frac{1}{2}$-inch intervals—a total of 9 squares—for the working pattern. As on the Honeybee, follow the instructions up to step 3, the curve within a square. Once again, flip and rotate (as on Honeybee step 4) and color to match the pattern.

This image shows the accurate grid, where four squares equals one large square on the basic grid. I quilted curved lines on the quilt flower and added tiny wooden shapes and a ladybird on the quilt shown.

Sheepfold

This needs a 4 x 4 grid, and as before, each square needs to be 2 inches. Many picture prints and borders are produced and the pictures of sheep seemed appropriate for this block. The print needs to be 4 inches square for this particular quilt, but if your chosen print is too small, add a border to make it up to the correct size. Color the grid as shown, and stitch the center block—there is no need to try to copy the design to the computer. Small hearts in the center of the corner squares add further interest.

Leaves

Here are two leaf designs, one of which uses foundation piecing and the other piecing. Each uses a 4 x 4 grid and the foundation pattern needs to print out to four inches for this quilt. To achieve this, use your accurate 6-inch grid with ½-inch intervals, treating each square as an inch, and print out to 200%. A foundation piercing layer order is shown here, as is the colored final. (For more in the method of foundation piecing, see page 78). To avoid using too many layers, this design uses two foundation-pieced triangles, divided diagonally. Each is separately numbered.

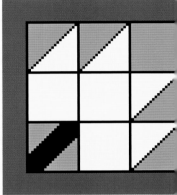

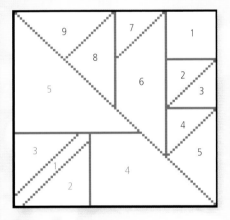

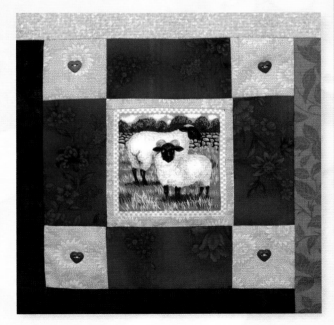

Foundation flower

This complete design needs to be drawn on an 8 x 8 grid, although only one quarter needs to be carefully mapped out. The actual flower takes up 6½ squares, and there is a ¼-inch border on each side which adds up to 7 inches. The spare inch makes the drawing easier and can be deleted when it is complete. As this quilt design actually needs an 8-inch square, the extra inch is taken up by having a ¾-inch border.

To make this quilt, the grid squares are counted in inches, so, to create an accurate foundation pattern, use your accurate ½-inch grid in ½ inches, counting each square as one inch, then print it out at 200%. Only one quarter of the pattern needs to be drawn.

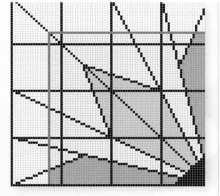

1 Enlarge your grid, then use the Line tool (╲) to draw in the stitching lines accurately. Start by drawing the diagonal as this helps to locate the other lines.

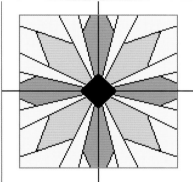

2 Then make three copies with the *Select* tool and *Edit* > *Copy* then *Edit* > *Paste* method. Use *Select* > *Image* > *Flip/Rotate* then choose *Flip Horizontal* for the first, flip the second both horizontally and vertically, then for the last one choose *Rotate by 180°*. Drag them to form the whole design, but when stitching, the four identical quarters are stitched separately then joined. The blue lines show the actual flower, the working outside the blue lines can be deleted to leave just the flower.

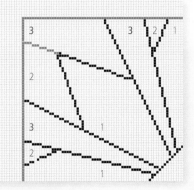

3 Depending on your confidence and experience with working from patterns, you may find it easier to delete the excess lines which makes the stitching lines clearer. Use the Line tool (╲) with a right click. Work out the stitching order and type in numbers following the typing instructions for the Leaf. Show the outer edge of the actual stitching with a colored line. When stitching, stitch each set of colored sections together, then join them.

Hen and her chicks and Crow's nest

Each of these blocks requires a 9 × 9 × 19 grid. The Hen and Her Chicks is composed of four nine patches and five squares, and the hen was appliquéd onto the center yellow square when the piecing was complete. The Crow's Nest has a nine-patch in the center.

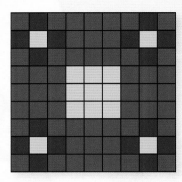

Hen and her chicks

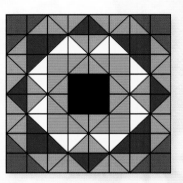

Crow's nest

Blossom Time

Blossom Time, also known as Spring Beauty, would fit well in the countryside quilt. Use an 8 × 8 × 19 basic grid here. This is a pieced block that would give an alternative for either the Honeybee, the Sheepfold or the Foundation Flower.

Hen and her chicks as stitched

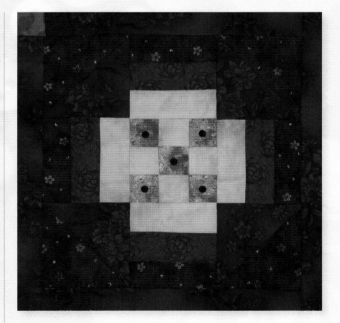

Crow's nest as stitched

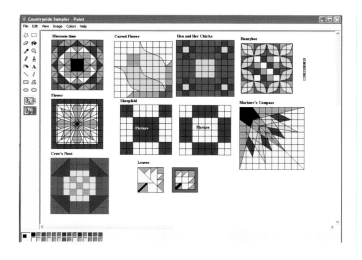

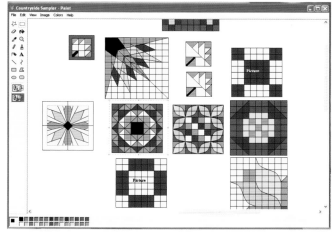

1 Now you should have all of the elements of your design ready in a single page. From left to right, the following designs are shown: Blossom Time, Curved Flower, Hen and her Chicks, Honeybee, Flower, Sheepfold, Mariner's Compass, Crow's Nest, and Leaves. It is time to make copies and drag these to different selections. Maybe another block is needed, perhaps all of the designs will not be used. The computer gives the opportunity to move, change, and alter colors without stitching at all. Then, when your design is complete, you can see exactly what stitching is needed and no time or materials are wasted.

3 Arrange the blocks roughly so that the colors and shapes are balanced. Move the blocks into rows in order to make the joining together more simple. Add piecing strips or border patterns between the blocks to make them fit.

2 When you have created a different layout, save it and try again with some more copies until you are happy with the result.

Christmas Hanging

This delightful quilted wall-hanging is made up of several blocks, each one a complete unit. This gives flexibility. One block would make a cushion or dinner mat, a row of stars would make a lovely table runner or a bell-pull, or a combination of several blocks would make a smaller hanging similar to the one shown in the pattern. I made each square of the pattern represent one inch and the finished size with the border measures 28 × 32 inches. Use the same grid squares throughout.

CD Files

The grids used in this folder are all in the *Grids* folder: *14x14x19*, *7x7x19*, *4x4x19*, *5x5x19*, and *6x6x19*.

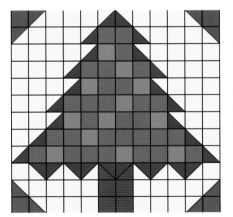

1 Copy the plans on pages 94-95 and move them to the top of the same screen. Select some festive colors and make a color strip on the screen that can be used each time you want to work on the design. Select a light, medium, and dark green, light and dark red, gold, brown, and a background color. Several different fabrics can be used for each computer color. For instance, the stitched hanging contains five different dark greens and five creamy backgrounds.

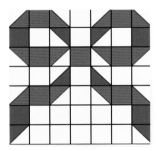

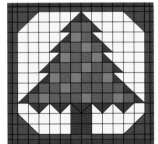

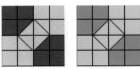

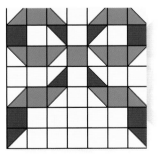

2 You now have a selection of patterns in the top store. Others can be added as you wish. Any or all of these can be copied, colored differently, flipped, and organized until you have a design you would like to stitch.

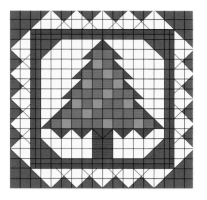

3 To add 2-inch "Prairie Points" to the tree design, first add at their base a two square border round the design, then draw the points at regular intervals. These points overlap at their base which adds a bit of an allowance for slightly inaccurate stitching as well as giving a cosy-looking theme. I could then begin to arrange the blocks using the Select tool ( ) to highlight them before dragging. It is useful to keep them in sections or rows as much as possible to make the stitching easier.

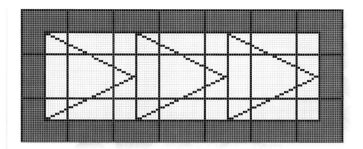

5 When I came to look again at the overall plan, I realized that if I deleted the green band under the parcels, then moved the parcel, bow, and star down one inch, it would make a straight band of patterns to stitch at the top, simplifying the joining of the blocks. This meant that the red border on the Flying Geese corners needed to be adjusted to fill the gap. Once that was done, the design was complete.

4 My design was going to be too wide, so I selected the side Prairie Points and clicked *Select > **Delete*** to remove them. When the blocks are more or less in place, the gaps need to be filled in. A colored strip works for small spaces, but larger gaps like the top right and left corners really need a border pattern. You can see the exact size that is required and experiment with different borders using the computer. In this case, the border pattern needs to be 3 inches deep and 7 wide, so you need to acquire a basic 3 × 7 grid. There are some borders on pages 42–43 that you could use, like the Flying Geese border, a very useful design for filling spaces.

6 Print off a pattern for the design and you'll have an accurate guide to follow. The black grid-lines on the pattern make it easy to see exactly what sizes of fabric are needed for the hanging, but don't forget to add your seam allowance to every piece. The diagram also shows how some of the blocks could be put together to make a bell-pull.

Variations

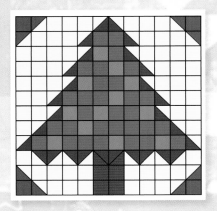

Tree pattern

Acquire a 14 × 14 × 19 grid. The central block is a variation of the Temperance Tree pattern. A clear pattern is shown on the CD, but the colored one shown here is not hard to follow. I worked this in squares, but longer strips of the background could be used to give fewer joins. Using the Line tool, copy the pattern for the tree, then color it (*see page 26*).

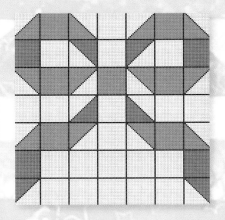

Bow

For the bows, use a 7 × 7 × 19 basic grid. Use the Line tool to draw the pattern, then copy and paste to obtain a second bow if you are following the plan for the hanging shown. Color one in light and dark green and one in reds. Select and drag to the top store and save.

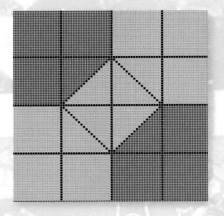

Parcel

Using a 4 × 4 × 19 basic grid, follow the same procedure for the parcels then color one in gold and dark green, and one in gold and one other color. Look at your fabrics, then make your choice. Add them to the top store and save.

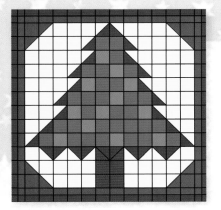

Copy and paste another row of squares all the way round the design, then use the Line tool and black to divide these in half to form the red and green border. When complete, select and drag the design to the top of the screen to form the top store, and save.

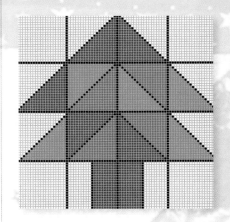

Small trees

Each of the trees in the row of little trees needs a 4 × 4 × 19 basic grid. Complete one tree then drag to the top store and save.

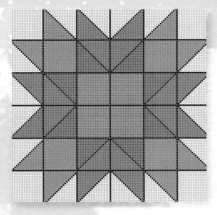

Christmas star

The Christmas Star needs a 6 × 6 × 19 basic grid. Using the Line tool, complete one pattern, then copy and paste a second one if needed. Color one mainly green with a red center and the other mainly red with a green center, then save your work.

Log cabin

Each Log Cabin block needs a 5 × 5 × 19 grid. Follow the pattern, place in the top store, and save. For more on log cabins, see page 52.

Final Design

The stitched quilt makes great use of festive colors, even if I do say so myself. Look out for fabrics with metallic gold for that extra sparkle.

Crazy Patchwork

This was a technique developed by early quilters in America which allowed fabrics of completely different fibers and weights to be used together by fastening them to a background base, overcoming the problems of stitching different fabrics in the same piece of work. The base can be of any firmly woven fabric because its only purpose is support; it will be completely covered up. Patches of all shapes and sizes are stitched onto the base randomly in a "crazy" design. Although originally it had a utilitarian purpose—enabling small fragments of fabric to be applied to worn blankets—in the 1880s it became a style of patchwork used to display embroidery skills. Sumptuous fabrics such as velvet, silk, and brocade were used and lace, ribbons, and beads were added, along with treasured fabrics from favorite items of clothing. Rich embroidery was worked along the edges of the patches and detailed motifs such as flowers, birds, people, butterflies, fans, and even cobwebs were worked on the patches.

CD Files

The 6-inch grid in ½-inch intervals can be derived from the CD at *Grids > 12x12x19*. Some computers can print grids at different sizes, but it's worth checking with a ruler. If necessary, draw your own grids using the instructions on page 24.

Crazy patchwork can be done using foundation piecing as shown on page 78, or the patches can be laid edge to edge on the base either randomly or following a design printed on the base fabric. The following wall hanging was done by using the computer to work out a design, then printing it to scale onto the base fabric in sections, which were then stitched together. Although it is a planned crazy patchwork design, following tradition, the edges are covered with either embroidery or bias tape and there is a fan design in the center. The fabrics used here are velvet, voile, cotton, silk, and polyester. Remnants from my daughter's wedding fabrics were used as the basis of this hanging. The burgundy centers were the actual Matron of Honour dress fabric, complete with beads; the other burgundy fabrics were possible swatches, the cream was the dress fabric, and the purple and black were extras. This design shows a center circle with a radiating fan surrounded by squares of crazy patchwork. Bias tape stitched along the dividing lines emphasizes these and forms definite segments like stained-glass leaded windows. Designing it on the computer gave me the opportunity to create a secondary pattern with the black lines on the squares surrounding the center design.

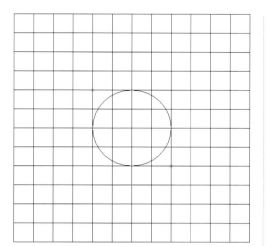

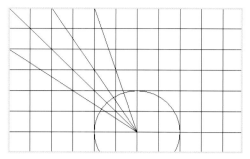

To create the fan center, first acquire an accurate 6-inch grid in ½-inch intervals either from your computer or by opening the relevant grid from the CD (see box on the previous page). This will give a 12-inch center foundation plan when printed at 200%. Placing a circle in the center not only gives a focal point to the design, it also makes the piecing easier as it eliminates the tiny points at the center. To draw the 4-inch circle, choose the Ellipse tool and place the cursor on the bottom-right corner of the top left 4 x 4 block, shown in the diagram by the green cross, then drag it across the center four squares to the top-left corner of the bottom-right 4 x 4 block, shown by the red cross, and release the mouse. A 4-inch circle will have been drawn in the center of the grid.

Zoom in to see the top-left quarter of the design, then use the Line tool (\) to mark segments from the edge to the center. This design uses 2-inch intervals.

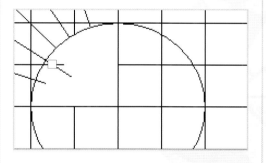

Erase the grid within the quarter circle using the Eraser tool (⌀), but leave the circle center horizontal and vertical lines as these are part of the segments.

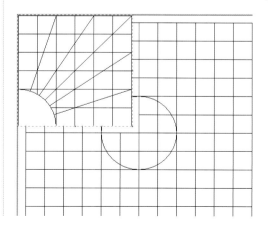

Select the segmented quarter circle, then copy and paste it. Click *Image > Flip/Rotate* and choose *Flip Horizontal* in the dialog box.

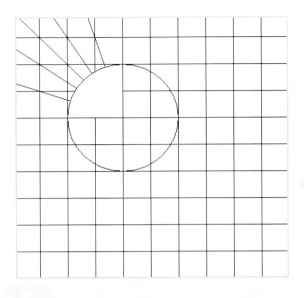

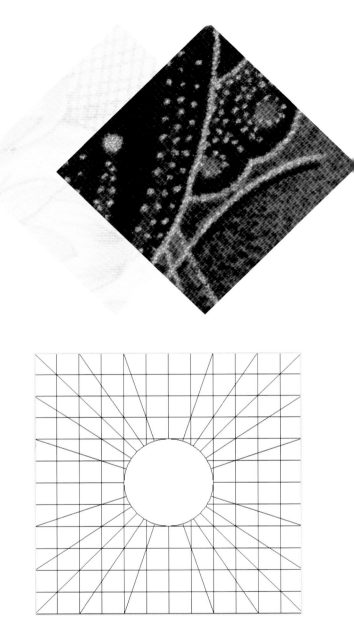

5 Finally, drag the copy to the top-right corner so that it lines up with the original grid.

A ribbon is added at the center of the design.

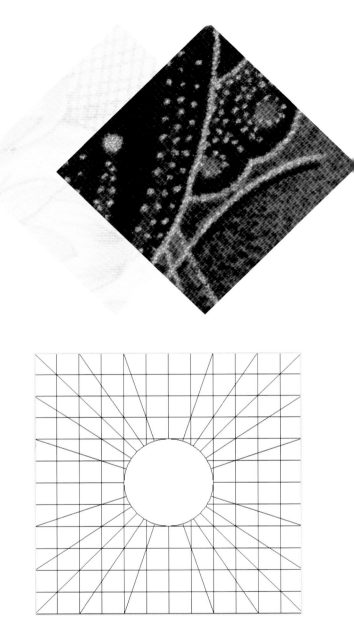

6 The top of the design is complete. Now use the Select tool (⬚) to highlight the whole top half of the pattern, and copy it as before. Click *Image* > **Flip/Rotate**, then choose *Flip Vertical* before positioning the resulting design over the lower half of the grid. Use the Eraser tool (✐) to clear the circle of all lines. The center square of the design is now complete.

Now acquire an accurate 3-inch grid in ½-inch intervals (which will print out a 6-inch foundation pattern at 200%). Make several copies of the grid using copy and paste, then use the Line tool (\) to draw straight lines dissecting the square. If you wish, you could make all 12 surrounding squares different. As I wanted a central shape in which to display the beaded fabric, I drew the lines close to the edges. I began with number 1 in the diagram, then developed this on other copies into 2 and 3, making it less pointed and more balanced with an pentagon in the center. I tried a different design with number 4, then took out the central line as this seemed to divide the block. I liked the shape of this design, number 5, with a quadrilateral in the center, as it seemed to form arrow shapes from left to right and bottom to top. I changed the lines slightly to make the shapes more even for number 6.

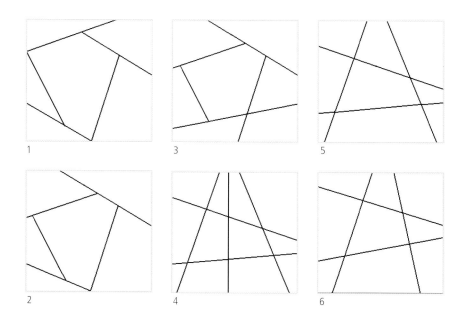

Some individual squares

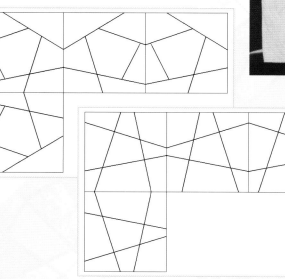

Try copying and pasting the blocks into a continuous horizontal border to see which works best. Copy and paste as usual, then horizontally flip the second square. Keep on in this manner; the next one will be the original, then the flipped design, and so on (work similarly in the vertical plane for the vertical border). I tried both the pentagon 3 and quadrilateral 6 as borders to see which worked best.

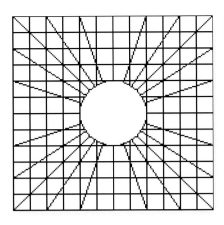

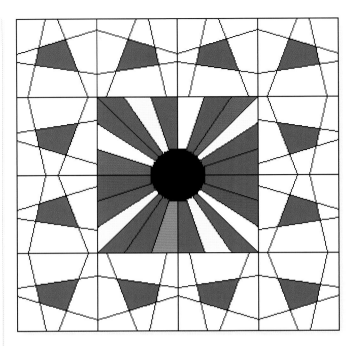

9 I chose the quadrilateral, but working on accurate grids at this size did not allow the whole wall hanging to be seen on the screen, so a basic grid needed to be drawn. Acquire a $12 \times 12 \times 12$ basic grid for the central design and select a $6 \times 6 \times 12$ basic grid for the squares. Copying the accurate designs, use the Line tool ($\searrow$) to create the two basic patterns.

11 When the design is complete, it can be colored with color from the Color Box or customized colors using the Fill With Color tool ($\circledast$). I colored the center fan and the centers of the squares, but chose to stitch the rest randomly, so have left blanks.

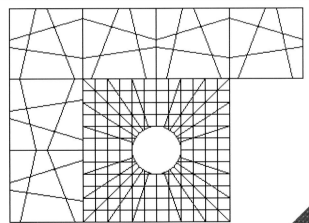

10 Using the copy and paste method, repeatedly duplicate the border design of your choice around the central fan. Flip horizontally, vertically, or both, as described in step 8.

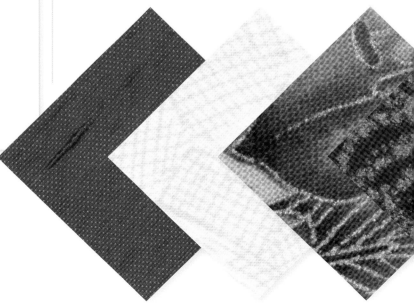

12 To print the foundation designs to full size, go to *File* >
Page Setup and change the Scaling box to 200% before
printing in the usual way (*File* > *Print*). Any number of identical
plans may be printed. Make sure the design is saved either on the
computer or a CD. Remember, if you are printing directly onto the
foundation papers, some of the plans will need to be flipped before
being printed. Refer to your complete design for this information.
If the plan is to be traced onto paper, the reverse of the printing
can be traced too.

Final design
Although the design is
not formed of traditional
symmetrical shapes, once
the blocks are combined
the overall quilt is very
pleasing to the eye.

Printing Out Onto Fabric

Products are now readily available to enable inkjet (or "Bubblejet" as Canon call it) printers to print from the computer directly onto fabric. This has given a new dimension to patchwork as it means that any photographs, scanned images, or text—in fact, any image that can be printed from the computer—can now be printed onto fabric, which can then form part of a quilt. The fabric images can be washed, ironed, and quilted as normal.

As with any patchwork, choice of fabric is paramount. For best results, 100% pure cotton or silk is needed and should be closely woven to prevent ink loss. Any finish must be washed out from the fabric as this will stop the ink penetrating.

Directly onto fabric

There are several ready-to-use sheets and rolls of pre-prepared fabric available which are simply fed through the printer one sheet at a time. These are made from white, finely woven cotton which has been treated with chemicals and has a backing. Each comes with specific instructions which are easy to follow and involve only an iron and mild detergent. For the quilt labels and the photograph in the Wedding cushion, Miracle Fabric Sheets from C. Jenkins and PhotoFabric from Blumenthal Craft were used. A disadvantage with these is that they are white, and although they could be fabric-painted after they have been printed, they cannot be dyed before the printing.

Inkjet printer

Inkjet printers have become very cheap, while still capable of producing detail far higher than necessary on fabric.

Fabric Transfer

If you wish to use your own fabric, try Bubble Jet Set 2000, which is used in conjunction with freezer paper and gives good results. This was used for the botanical flower illustrations in the Flower quilt.

To use Bubble Jet Set 2000, first cut a piece of freezer paper to a size that will go through your printer, then cut a piece of fabric slightly larger than this. Pour the liquid into a flat tray, then soak the fabric for five minutes until it is saturated with the solution. Try to keep the fabric as flat as possible and not scrunch it up. Take the fabric from the solution and let it dry flat, either by hanging it up or laying it on a towel. When it is dry, iron the back of the fabric to the smooth side of the freezer paper and use your rotary cutter to trim the fabric to the size of the paper. This is then ready to be used.

When printing, use normal inkjet cartridges for the best results. If it is possible with your printer's software (the menu that appears after you choose Print from Paint), increase the ink level to give a slightly darker result.

Feed the prepared sheets through the printer singly with the fabric on the printing side. When the design has printed, it must be allowed to dry. I have found that leaving it for the recommended time is not always enough, and it is best to leave it overnight.

The backing paper or freezer paper is then removed. At this stage some products require the fabric to be heat-set with an iron and then rinsed well with a mild detergent and cool water. Other products, including Bubble Jet Set 2000, must not be ironed until after they have been well rinsed and dried. For the best results, a mild detergent should be used. There are products on the market, such as Bubble Jet Rinse, made especially for this purpose.

When the fabric has been washed, do not wring it out, but allow it to drip dry or lay it flat on a towel to dry. To make the process quicker, it can be blown dry with a hairdryer. The printed fabric can then be used as any other.

These products have made fabrics printed with your own photographs or pictures very easy to achieve. The ready-prepared products are more expensive per sheet, but are convenient, especially for small items like quilt labels, but the Bubble Jet Set 2000, which takes slightly longer to use, is cheaper where a number of items are to be printed and it can be poured back into the bottle to use again. I have found all of the products work well following the manufacturer's instructions and none is difficult to use.

Printing materials

Inkjet transfer paper, special fabrics for direct printing, and fixing agents are all parts of the quilter's toolkit.

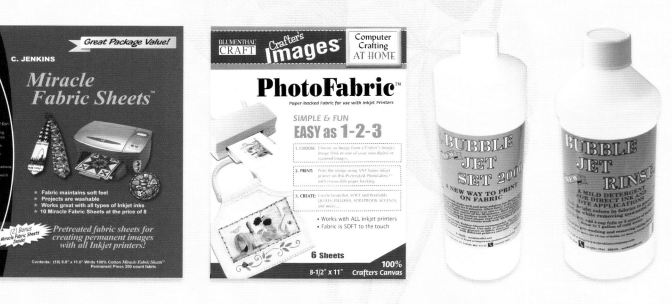

Printing Out Onto Fabric: Flower Quilt

I have always liked botanical illustrations, so for this quilt I found paintings by Pierre Joseph Redouté and printed them in grayscale instead of color. (When you are sourcing images for your designs, make sure you don't infringe anyone's copyright, for example by downloading them from the internet without permission.) In Paint, change the files from color to grayscale by clicking *Image > Attributes* and choosing the *Black and White* box. Once the work has been changed to black and white, only new sections will be in color as the program will not reverse the procedure.

CD Files

This project uses a 12 × 12 × 11 grid, as found on the CD in the file called *Grids > 12x12x11*.

For this quilt I didn't want a symmetrical look, so I chose a range of pictures that are different sizes. If you prefer, you can make them all the same size. Their dimensions can be adjusted by using *Select > Image > Stretch and Skew* then altering the percentage of the horizontal and vertical stretch options. To keep the same proportions, the horizontal and vertical adjustment should be the same. Using this method, all the pictures can be lined up on one screen and adjusted before printing.

In order to use my own choice of fabric, I used the Bubble Jet Set method described on page 102, printing in grayscale on a mottled cream cotton. This gave an old look to the pictures, so, to keep the same feeling, I selected fabrics with subdued tones for the rest of the quilt.

1 The first step in planning the quilt is to acquire the pictures. In this case it was six botanical illustrations, but it could be any selection of pictures, photographs, or subjects. Print them onto fabric using one of the methods outlined previously, then trim them to size, remembering the ¼-inch seam allowance. It makes life easier for placing them in the grid if the stitched size can be either a whole or half inch.

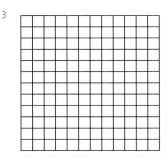

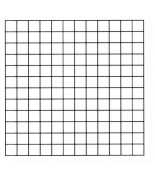

Ready for flower picture sizes

2 In order to plan the design using the computer, a basic grid with an odd number of pixels is needed. I used a 12 × 12 × 11 grid. Either draw this using the Line tool (\) or use the one on the CD. Make it as large as you need for your quilt by copying and pasting the squares. This flower quilt is 48 × 36 inches in a Landscape orientation. Cut and paste a strip of the grid to act as a color key. This will save the colors from one designing session to the next when the computer is switched off, as Paint reverts to the default palette.

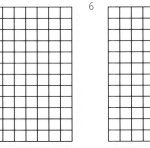

1

3

5

2

4

6

3 At the same time, create a 12 × 12 × 11 grid for each picture to be used. If it is necessary to extend the working area, use *Image* > **Attributes** and enlarge the *Width* and/or *Height* properties.

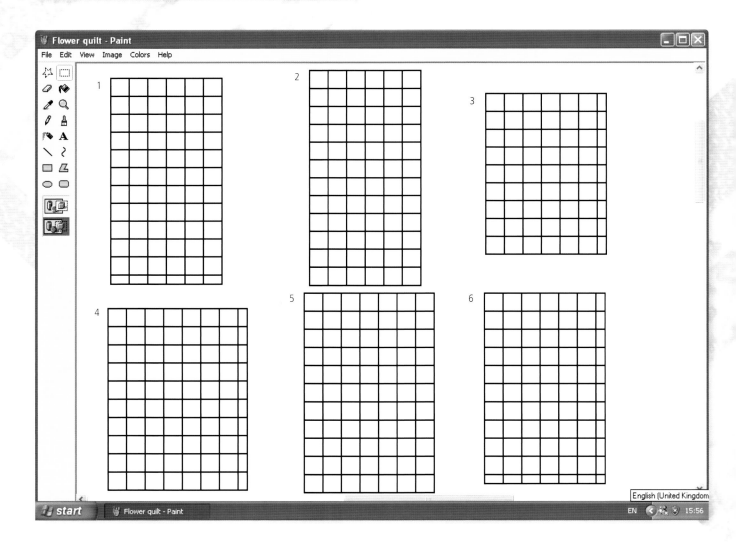

4 Number each of the pictures on the back with a piece of masking tape, then use the Text tool (**A**) to number each picture grid. Measure the size of the picture and use the Select tool (▱) to highlight the excess grid squares before clicking *Select > Delete* to clear them. The grid squares should now correspond to the picture sizes. (If the picture is greater than 12 × 12 × 11, add more squares to the grid using the copy and paste method. To create the half inches, zoom into the grid and use the Line tool to draw the half-inch line on the sixth pixel.)

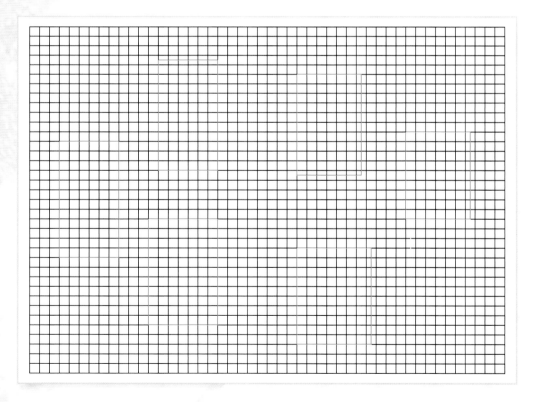

Moving frames later

To alter the placing of a frame later, choose black, and, using the Fill With Color tool (🖱), click on the frame that needs changing. The frame will change to black and become part of the grid again. Copy and paste another copy in a different place.

5 Using the Select tool (⬚) as above, highlight and delete the inside grid of the picture to leave a frame which is the same size as the picture and will represent the picture in the plan. Choose a color then use the Fill With Color tool (🖱) to click on the frame to change its color.

6 Be sure that you are working in transparent background mode. To do this, choose the *Select* tool (⬚), then choose the lower of the two selection options at the bottom of the toolbox.

7 Now use the *Select* tool (⬚) to highlight one of the frames and click *Edit* > **Copy**. Click *Edit* > **Paste**, then drag and place the copy onto the main quilt grid in the position where you intend it to be. The transparent background set in step 6 means that only the colored frame will be superimposed on the grid and any grid lines inside the frame will still be visible. (Choosing *Edit* > **Undo** or pressing Ctrl+Z will undo up to the last three moves if the frames are incorrectly placed.)

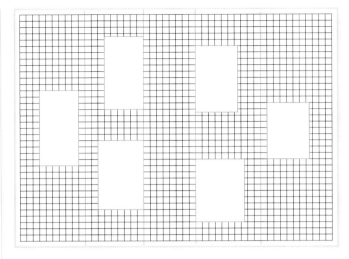

Save the design. Now carefully highlight the inside of the frames with the Select tool (┊┄┊), then click *Select* > **Delete** to remove the lines across the centers of the frames. This makes the balance of the design clearer. The frames may still need some adjustment if you are not happy with it, so revert to a saved version.

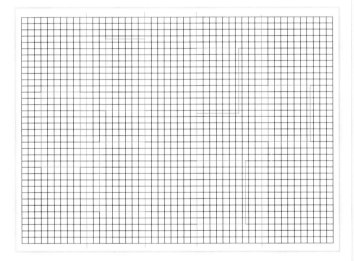

Where there are lines left that are extra to the grid, for example ½-inch lines, select the Line tool (\) or Pencil tool (✎) tool and right-click to delete them. Spacing the flower frames evenly and fairly symmetrically will give a balanced design that is pleasing to the eye. To make the piecing more straightforward, line up the edges of the pictures either vertically or horizontally. It may be helpful to use the Line tool (\) to draw a colored line for the planned piecing. I have shown this in blue and will piece the design in five vertical strips.

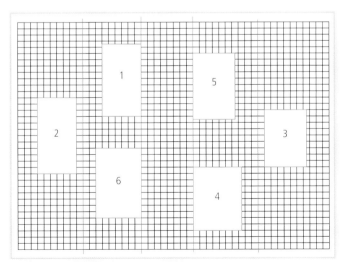

I found that the right-hand frame was too high up, so I selected and dragged it to a lower position, then completed the grid using the *Line* tool (\). Use the *Text* tool (**A**) to number the blank frames so that the plan is easy to refer to in the future.

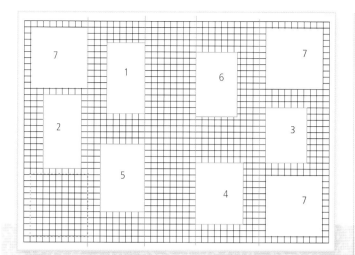

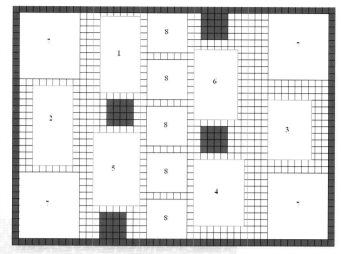

11 I decided that this quilt should have four plain quilted blocks, one in each corner. To plan the size for these, use the same selection and deleting method from step 9 to leave a space. Try different sizes, making use of *Edit* > **Undo** or Ctrl+Z as necessary. To replace the quilted corners with a pieced block or to make each corner have a different block, take the size of the block that you want to use and clear a corresponding space. Number or name each one as you do so.

13 There were four obvious blank spaces in the design which I decided to fill with 16-patch blocks. However, in order to fit these in, it was necessary to use Select and drag to move the picture numbered one up two squares, number six down one square and five up by one square. The 16-patch blocks are shown in purple. To make this easier for piecing, the blue piecing lines were adjusted by selecting the Line tool (\) then right-clicking over the original to erase the line, before drawing it back using the same tool and left clicking. Stripes in random colors from the toning fabrics are to fill the rest of the design. Choose or customize colors for the design (*see page 26*) remembering to fill in the color key strip. I have given the quilt a dark border using the Fill With Color tool (🖌).

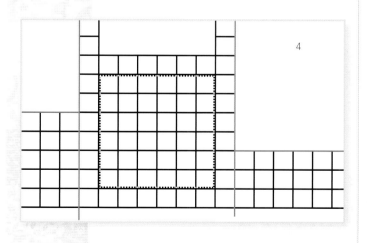

12 In the same way, I planned five Snowball blocks to be stitched in the center of the design by selecting and deleting spaces.

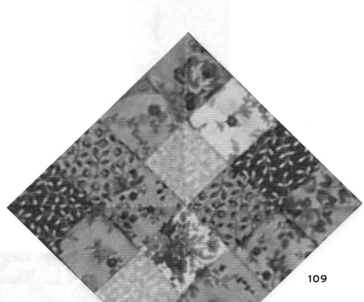

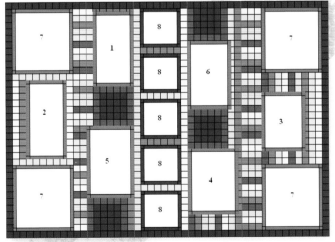

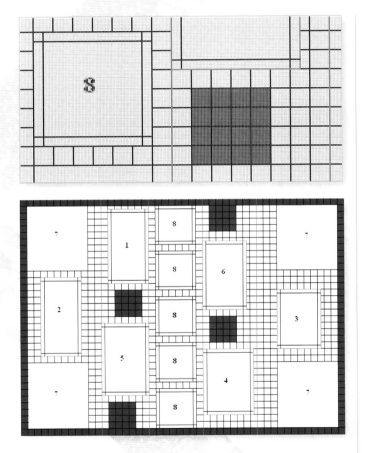

14 Half-inch borders need to be added to the picture and Snowball blocks using the Line tool (↘). Notice that the borders come inside the original block lines so that the overall sizes of the blocks remain the same.

15 Color the borders, then add stripes of random colors, both vertical and horizontal. There is also room for design changes: I selected and dragged the section, including 6 and 4, up half an inch so it would be easier to stitch. The grid lines were adjusted using the Line tool (↘).

The final quilt

The final product elegantly combines printed
images of flowers with the traditional feel of real
patchwork, using diamond and zig-zag quilting.

Diamond Wedding wall hanging

To add to the anniversary gifts, a wall hanging celebrating a Diamond Wedding needed a photograph of the wedding 60 years ago for its center. This was secreted away, many months ago. The picture first needs to be scanned or imported onto the computer into Paint, or your choice of graphics application.

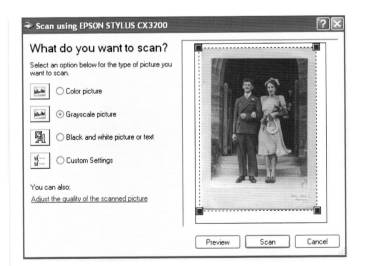

1 To import from a scanner, open Paint and place the photograph in the scanner. Go to *File > **From Scanner or Camera*** and an options box will appear. The exact details of this box differ from scanner to scanner, but the principles are the same. You can choose to scan in color or grayscale, then choose preview and mark the area to be scanned (much like selecting an area of a quilt pattern before moving it).

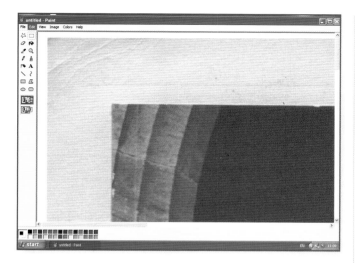

2   When you have pressed OK, the top-left corner of the scan will appear, looking far too large. In order to work on the image, you will need to reduce the picture size and then increase it back again before printing. To reduce the image, go to *Image > Stretch and Skew*, then alter the horizontal and vertical settings to 25% and press OK.

3   The picture will become much smaller. If you need to reduce it even more, change the percentage again. To increase the working area, go to *Image > Attributes* and alter the *Width* and *Height* settings. The white working area will extend. At this stage you may edit the picture. To facilitate this, you may need to highlight the image using the Select tool ( ) and drag the picture elsewhere on the page to provide more room. I first needed to delete some of the frame by selecting it then clicking *Select > Delete*. If the image is large, it may need to be edited in sections by scrolling up and down or right and left.

Selecting in parts

If the image is too large to select in one go, you may need to move it in two pieces. If the image is to be moved up, Select and drag the top half upwards first, then Select and drag the bottom to rejoin it. If it is to be moved down, Select and drag the bottom half first. Similarly, to move to the right or left, move the right or left half first. Make sure you use the Select tool (▦) in transparent mode (see page 19) to enable you to make sure that the two halves butt together and do not overlap.

4 In order to see how the picture will look on a Letter or A4-sized page, go to *File* > ***Print Preview***. To return to the main screen, press Close at the top of the screen.

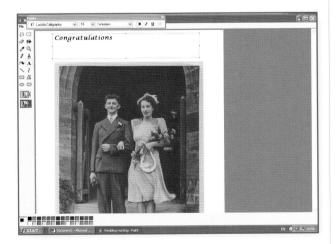

5 To add text to the image, use the Text tool to draw a box in which the text is to be written, then type your text. Once the writing is complete, you can use the Select tool (▦) and drag to move part or the whole of it, so the initial positioning need not be the final result and is not crucial.

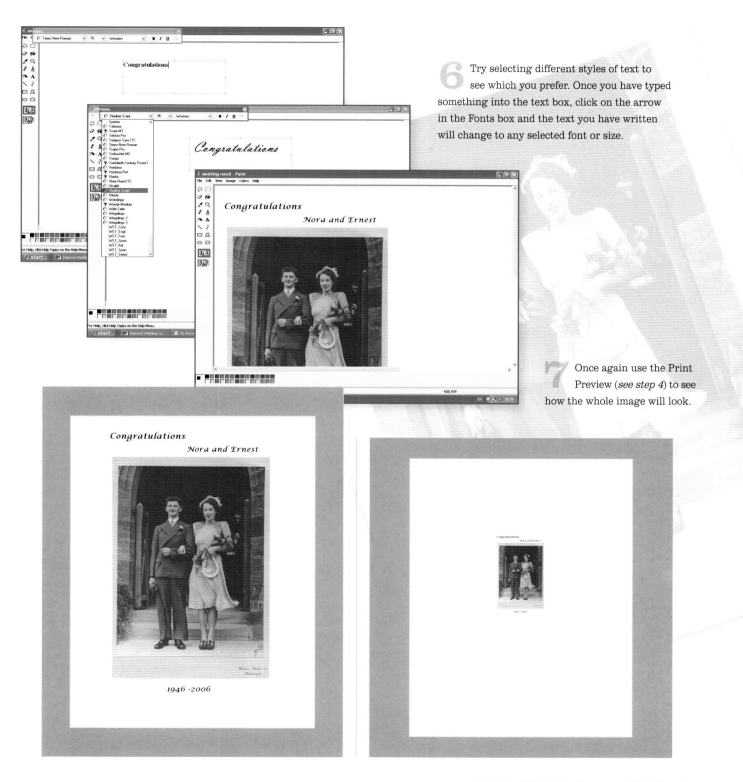

6 Try selecting different styles of text to see which you prefer. Once you have typed something into the text box, click on the arrow in the Fonts box and the text you have written will change to any selected font or size.

7 Once again use the Print Preview (*see step 4*) to see how the whole image will look.

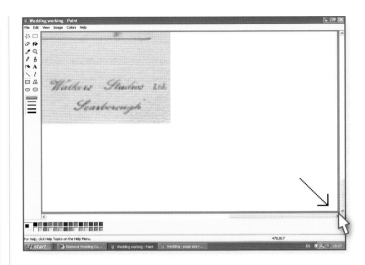

8 To see how large the printed page will be (the area with picture on) go to *Image > **Attributes***. The page size will be shown. The measurement here shows that this page is 2.93 inches wide and 2.93 inches high.

9 To find the measurement for the image size, first highlight the whole picture with the Select tool (⬚), then drag the design to the top-left corner of the page.

10 Scroll to the bottom-right corner of the page. There is a blue image-resize handle on the corner, indicated by the arrow. It is quite difficult to see and appears as a blue dot. Place the cursor on this until the cursor changes to a double-ended arrow, then drag up and to the left until the page is in line with the size of image you wish to print.

11 Open the *Image > **Attributes*** box to see the printed page size. It is now 1.69 by 2.82 inches. (These numbers will, of course, vary depending on your picture.)

12 Look at the Print Preview again. This is too small; it needs to be twice the size to fit into the 5 × 7 inch center with a suitable border. To enlarge the printed size and still keep the picture's detail, go to *File* > ***Page Setup*** and adjust the scaling percentage. I changed it to 200%. Again, I used the Print Preview facility to see how it would look on the Letter (or A4) page.

13 When it is correct, place the pre-prepared fabric sheet in the printer, go to *File* > ***Print***, choose the printer and click Print. It may be useful to try a print first on a piece of paper before using the fabric.

14 To create a patchwork design including a printed image, first decide on the size for the centre, in this case, 5 × 7 inch portrait style. Acquire a 14 × 14 × 12 basic grid, either by drawing one using Copy and Paste from your computer, or by opening the 14 × 14 × 12 grid from the CD. If your design needs a larger grid, acquire one grid then *Select* > *Edit* > ***Copy*** and *Edit* > ***Paste*** grids adjacent to each other until you attain the size required.

Digital photos

As an alternative to scanning your picture, you might want to use a picture from a digital camera. Unlike scanned pictures, these files are very ethereal, having never really "existed" in solid print form. In other words, be careful. Before you do anything else, copy your original photograph in your computer's Explorer window (or Finder on a Mac).

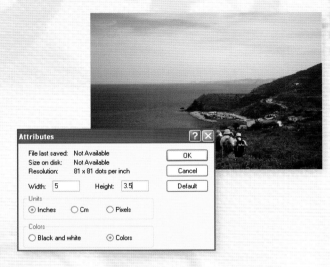

1 To open a picture from the computer, first open Paint and then, to choose a specific size for the image, go to *Image* > *Attributes* and set the width and height. Click OK. The working area will be set for this size. Press Ctrl+A to select the area, or do this with the Select tool (▭).

2 The working area will be set for this size. Press Ctrl+A to select the area, or do this with the Select tool (▭).

3 Click *Edit* > *Paste From* to open a pasting dialog box. Locate the image that you want to insert (you can access all the files stored on your computer's drives from here).

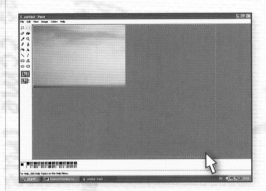

4 When you find the picture you're looking for, simply double-click on it. The image will appear and, unless it is smaller than your planned print area, only the top-left corner will be visible. Place the cursor on the small blue dot, which is a resize handle, at the bottom-right corner of the image until it changes to a double-ended arrow, then drag the image to the selected area and release the mouse.

5 If you want to create space around the image to work with—perhaps to add text—go to *Image* > *Attributes* and increase the width and height. The imported image can then be selected and moved as in the previous example.

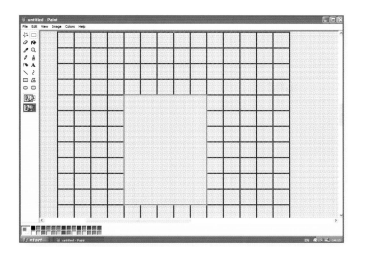

15 Using the *Line* tool (\) and a color other than black, draw the outline of the center image, then use *Select* > **Delete** to remove the center. The patchwork design can then be planned around this empty box.

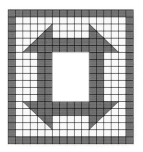

The Monkey Wrench

16 The Monkey Wrench block is being used here, but you could choose another variation.

Pattern Variations

There are many other suitable designs, such as Five-Patch Corner, Friendship Block, Kitty Corner, Sage Bud of Wyoming, and Squirrel in a Cage.

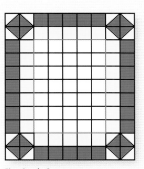

Five-Patch Corner

Friendship Block

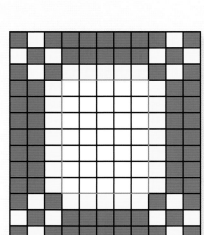

Kitty Corner

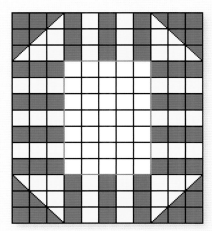

Sage Bud of Wyoming

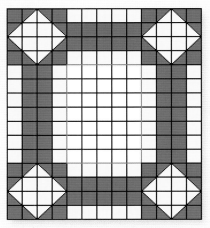

Squirrel in a Cage

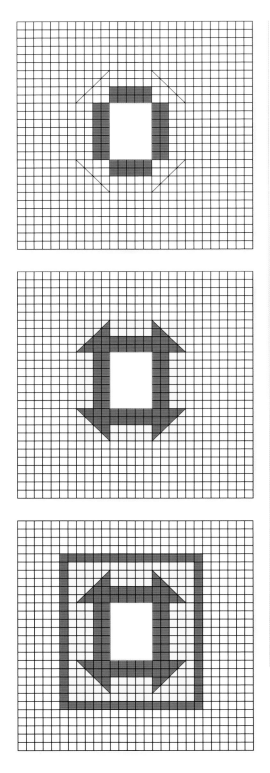

Final revisions

The smaller design would make a lovely lavender wall hanging to sit on a dressing table or hang on a ribbon. I changed the coloring to lavender colors and made up this design.

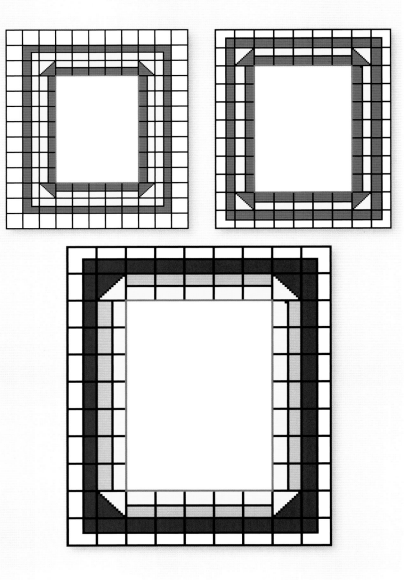

17 On the grid, use the Line tool (⟍) with black to draw the pattern lines, then choose the colors and use the Fill With Color tool (🎨) to color the design. Add borders or further patchwork to the design until it is complete.

Complete
The completed wall-hanging, which now takes pride of place in Nora and Ernest's house.

Individual Quilt Labels

Thanks to the ability to print directly to fabric, you can put the final touch to your quilt by giving it a personal label. Adding a label to your quilt or wall-hanging completes it, just like signing a letter or painting or autographing a book. It also provides information for anyone looking at it in the future, whether it is tomorrow, next year, or in the next century! The name of the stitcher and the quilter should be included, together with the date and anything else you feel is appropriate. It is also a nice idea to sign the label using a fine indelible pen.

1 First you need to acquire an image, and this can be done by any digital means—a scanner, a digital camera, via the internet, or some royalty-free clip art from a CD; you could even draw your own designs on the computer. If your quilt is not just for personal use, please remember that other people's images and designs are automatically copyright to them and you will need to seek permission to use them. There are many books and CDs for sale with a wide range of suitable designs, including wreaths and frames, which only need the text adding into the space. The Basket label and the Diamond Wedding Violets were taken from the copyright-free Dover publication *Old-Time Fruits and Flowers Vignettes in Full Color.* Poppies was made using a photograph taken by the side of the highway in East Yorkshire, England.

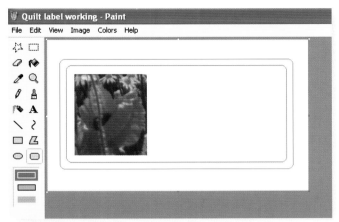

2 Scan the photograph you wish to use or transfer it directly from the camera using *File* > ***From Scanner or Camera***. Then choose the Select tool (⬚) and highlight a portion of the image. Press Ctrl+C (or click *Edit* > ***Copy***) to copy that selection to the clipboard.

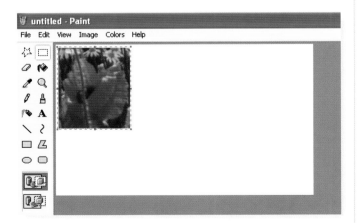

3 In Paint, create a new image and use *Image* > ***Attributes*** to set the size for your label. For this label I chose 5 × 3 inches. As soon as your document is open, click *Edit* > ***Paste*** to add the design from the clipboard. Select and drag to move the image to the correct position to allow for the text.

4 Adding one or more line borders to the label gives unity to the design (or sections within it). First use the *Pick Color* tool (✐) to choose a color from the image (*see page 26*). Select the *Rounded Rectangle* tool (⬭) and then choose the thickness of line from the bottom of the toolbox. Finally to draw the line place the cursor at the top-left corner of your planned border, then drag to the bottom right and release. To have a double border, repeat the same procedure.

Scale to fit

When you paste your scanned image into Paint (see step 3), it will appear in the top-left corner of the working area. If the image is too big, you have two options. If the size is almost right, place the cursor on the blue resize handle, appearing as a blue dot, at the bottom-right corner of the picture and drag the cursor diagonally towards the top-left corner, then release the mouse when your image is the right size. You do need to take care to keep the proportions accurate. Remember, *Edit* > *Undo* will take it back to the original size. If the size is much too large, go to *Image* > *Stretch and Skew* and alter the size.

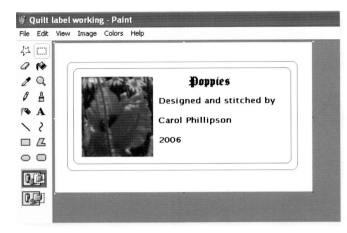

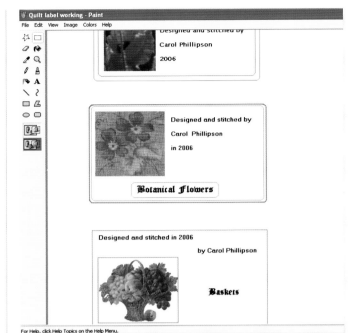

For Help, click Help Topics on the Help Menu.

5 Now it's time to add some text to the design. Click on the Text tool (**A**) and drag the cursor to define the position of the text. Choose the type of text and size from the Fonts box which appears automatically, then type your text. (It can always be repositioned later using the Select tool (⬚) and dragging.) You can continue to play around with alternative type styles while the text box is visible. All of the text in the text box will change. I have used Old English Text MT size 14 for the name of the quilt and MS Sans Serif size 10 for the information. A separate text box needed to be drawn for each.

6 This could now be printed using an inkjet or bubblejet printer onto a pre-prepared fabric sheet (*see page 102*). Several labels can be printed on one sheet: simply use *Image > Attributes* to enlarge the working area to match the size of your paper and duplicate the label by selecting it and copying using the *Edit > Copy* then *Edit > Paste* method to fill the page.

7 This particular label only applies to one quilt, so instead of copying and pasting it ready for printing, I saved it on the enlarged page to be printed with some others later. For the other labels, the same procedure was followed, but for the Botanical flowers label, a piece of the actual fabric was placed in the scanner and imported into Paint using *File > From Scanner or Camera*.

Austrian Summer

Memories of a wonderful holiday
Thank you

Designed and stitched by Carol Phillipson in 2006

Designed and stitched by

Carol Phillipson

in 2006

Botanical Flowers

Violets

Stitched to celebrate the Diamond Wedding on September 22nd 2006

Ernest and Nora Pobgee

With Love

Poppies

Designed and stitched by

Carol Phillipson

2006

Folk Art

Designed as a foundation-pieced wall-hanging

by Carol Phillipson

in 2005

Wheelbarrow

While selecting the Baskets image, I found a
lovely picture of a wheelbarrow full of violets
which seemed perfect for the label for the
Diamond Wedding hanging, so I created this
label in the same way as the others.

Index

Add to Custom Colors 26-27

Adobe 14

Air Castle 66, 68

Airbrush 17

Alternative Trees 74

Anna's Basket 47

Apple Macintosh 14-15, 118

appliqué 39-40, 49-50, 68, 84, 86, 90

Attributes 21, 24, 35, 65, 104-5, 113, 116, 118, 123-24

Baby blocks 72

Baby quilt 76-77

Basket of Diamonds 47

Basket label 122, 125

Basket wall-hanging 11, 46-51

beads 96, 99

Bear's Paw quilt 11, 34-37

bed covers 76

bell-pull 92-93

bias tape 49, 96

Birds in Flight 54

Black and White box 104

blanket 96

block stitching order 52

blocks 8-11, 22, 46, 56, 92

Blossom Time 84, 90-91

Blue Star 10

Blumenthal Craft 102

borders 10-11, 33, 36, 38-46, 56, 66-68, 79, 89, 93, 123

botanical illustrations 104

Bow 94

Broken Sugar Bowl 47

Brush 17

Bubble Jet Rinse 103

Bubble Jet Set 103-4

Bubblejet printers 102, 124

buttons 50, 69, 84

Canon 102

cartridges 103

CD files see templates

CDs 20, 27

Chevron 55, 60

Christmas hanging 92-95

Christmas Star 94

Church design 78-79

Church Window 70, 73

Circle tool 17

Clam 77

Clay's Choice 66, 68

Clear 33

clip art 122

Coffin 70, 72

Color box 9, 23, 25-27, 35, 51, 100

color key 64-65, 105, 109

color plan 28

color procedure 26-27, 52

Color Selection box 17

color wheel 9

color-coding 46

compass design 84-85

complementary colors 9

cool colors 9

copies 48, 53

Copy 9-10, 18, 23, 27, 30-31, 35, 40, 44, 49, 54, 61, 72, 81, 89, 107, 117, 123-24

copyright 122

cornerstones 39-40

Countryside quilt 6, 84-91

Courthouse Square 10, 32-33

Crazy Patchwork 96-101

Crow's Nest 84, 90-91

Curved Flower 87, 91

Curved Line tool 17, 86

curves 8, 84

cushions 92

Custom 19, 22, 32

customizing colors 26-27, 56, 61, 65, 71, 76, 85, 100, 109

Cut 18

default palette 105

Define Custom Colors 26

Delete 27, 35, 71, 93, 106, 108, 113, 119

diamond blocks 72

Diamond Wedding Violets 122

Diamond Wedding wall hanging 112-21, 125

digital cameras 118, 122

dinner mat 92

double borders 123

dyeing 102

Edit Colors 26-27

Ellipse tool 17, 49, 76, 97

embroidery 50, 96

enlarging patterns 53

Eraser tool 17, 28, 33, 52, 71, 97-98

Explorer 118

fabric printing 102-11, 122

fabric types 96, 102

fan 96-97, 100

Fill With Color tool 9, 11, 17, 25, 27-28, 31-33, 35-36, 40, 44, 48, 52-53, 61, 64-66, 68, 71, 80, 85, 100, 107, 109, 120

Finder 118

Five-Patch Corner 119

fixing agents 103

Flip Horizontal 72, 82, 85, 89, 97

Flip Vertical 85, 98

Flip/Rotate 9, 16, 28, 39-40, 44, 53, 68, 72, 82, 86, 89, 97-98

Flower 84, 89-91

Flower quilt 103-11

Flying Geese 42, 93

focal point 97

Fonts box 115, 124

foundation paper 78-79, 82

foundation piecing 78-84, 88, 96

Free-Form select 17

freeware 14

freezer paper 103

Friendship 119

From Scanner or Camera 112, 122, 124

Fruit Basket 47, 51

Full Off Center 55

Grandmother's Flower Garden 70, 73

grayscale 104, 112

gridline experiments 81

grids 22-25, 42-43, 46, 49-50, 52, 72, 80-81

hair-dryer 103

half-square triangles 11, 30, 46, 54

handles 46, 49-50

hangings 30, 32, 46, 60, 64, 74-75, 80, 92, 96, 112

heat-setting 103

Hen and Her Chicks 84, 90-91

Herringbone quilt 8

Hexagon wall hanging 9, 70-75

hexagons 8, 70-71, 75

Hidden Star 66, 68

Hole in One 10

Honeybee 84, 86-87, 90-91

honeycomb effect 70

Horizontal Scroll bar 17

House 80-81

individual quilt labels 122-25

inkjet printers 102-3, 124

internet 122

ironing 102-3

isometric grids 72

Jenkins, C. 102-3

junctions 39

keyboard shortcuts 16, 28, 35-36, 53, 76, 109, 118, 123

Kitty Corner 119

labels 122-25

Landscape orientation 105

lap-quilts 50

Large Size 19

Lavender hanging 120

Leaves 84, 88-89, 91

lettering 82

Line tool 11, 17, 23, 25, 27-28, 30, 32-36, 40, 48, 50-51, 60, 65-66, 70-72, 76, 80-81, 85, 89, 94, 97, 99, 105-6, 108, 119-20
Log Cabin 42, 56, 95
Log Cabin Poppy quilt 9-11, 52-55

Mac OS X 15
Macs see Apple Macintosh
Magnifier 17
Mariner's Compass 84-86, 91
master copies 28, 68
master plans 85
May Basket 47
Medallion quilt 8, 53
Menu bar 16-17
Microsoft 14, 16-17
Miracle Fabric Sheets 102
mirror images 39
mitred borders 39-40
Monkey Wrench 119
moving frames later 107
Mystery Basket 47

Noon Star 65, 67-68
Normal Size 19
numbering 79, 82

octagons 8
Off Center 55
on-point designs 10, 22, 32-33, 46-47, 50, 63, 65
one-patch designs 8, 60
Option box 17

Page Setup 21, 101, 117
page size 116
Paint 6, 14, 16-17
Parcel 94
Paste 9-10, 18, 23, 27, 30-31, 35, 40, 44, 49, 54, 61, 72, 81, 89, 107, 117, 123-24
Paste From 118
patterns 92-93
PCs 14

Pencil tool 17, 40, 49, 51, 60, 108
PhotoFabric 102
photographs 112
Photoshop Elements 14, 24
Pick Color tool 17, 31, 35, 49, 64-65, 123
piecing 68, 70, 78-84, 86, 88, 91, 96-97
Pineapple Block 55
Pinwheels 54, 78-79
pixels 23, 40
planning 39, 48, 64, 71, 75, 79-80, 104
Playmat 76-77
Polygon tool 17
Poppy quilt 56-59
pouncing 51
Prairie Points 93
pre-prepared fabric 102, 117, 124
previews 48
Print 101, 117
Print from Paint 103
Print Preview 21, 114-15, 117
printers 21, 79, 85, 102-3, 124
printing 102-11, 122

quilt labels 122-25
quilted basket center 50-51
quilts 6-7, 34, 52, 84, 104

Rainbow Squares 8, 11, 30-31
resize handle 118
Rectangle tool 17, 25, 33, 40
rectangles 8, 70, 72
Redouté, P.J. 104
reducing patterns 53
repetitive coloring 77
ribbon 96
right-clicking 51, 71, 82, 89, 109
Rising Star 65, 67-68
rotary cutter 28, 103
Rotate by Angle 77, 86
Rounded Rectangle tool 17, 123
Royal Star 65, 68

Sage Bud of Wyoming 119
sashing 9-11, 34, 36, 38-41, 44-45, 48, 62, 68
Save 20, 31
Save As 20
saving 27
scale to fit 123
Scaling box 101
scallop borders 77
scanners 112, 118, 122
Scrappy Herringbone 60-63
Scrappy quilt 77
Sea Storm 55
Seahorses quilt 55
seam allowance 28, 76, 104
Seashore 14
Seasons hanging 78, 80-83
secondary patterns 10, 44, 96
Select tool 17, 21, 23, 27, 31, 33, 35-36, 40, 44, 48, 53-54, 61, 68, 71, 81, 89, 93, 98, 106-9, 113-14, 116, 118, 123-24
selecting in parts 114
settings 10
Seven-Patch Bear's Paw quilt 34-37
shareware 14
Sheepfold 84, 88, 90-91
Shell 77
Show Grid 19, 22
Small Tree 94
Snowball 109-10
Spool variation 67-68
Spring Beauty 90
square borders 39
squares 8, 47, 70, 72
Squares within a Square 42, 67-68
Squirrel in a Cage 119
Star 42, 92, 94
Star wall hanging 64-69
stencils 51, 82
Straight Furrows 55
Streak o' Lightning 55
Stretch and Skew 53, 104, 113
Strippy quilt 7-8, 11, 42, 44
Sugar Bowl of Cherries 47

Sun 84
Sunshine and Shadow 54

table runner 92
Temperance Tree 94
templates 22, 30, 32, 34, 38, 46, 49, 52, 56, 60, 62, 64, 70, 72, 76, 78, 80, 84-87, 92, 96, 104
Text tool 17, 82, 106, 108, 114, 124
texture 48
Thistle 53
Thousand Pyramids 8
three-dimensional looks 50, 72
Toolbar/box 16, 40, 86, 107, 123
tracing 51
transfer paper 103
Transparent mode 19, 23
Trees 67-68, 73-74, 80, 94
triangles 8, 70, 72, 88
Trip Around the World 8
Tumbling blocks 72
type styles 124

Undo 28, 35-36, 40, 72, 86, 107
utilitarian patchwork 96

variations 35, 40, 47, 54-55, 66-68, 77, 83, 94-95, 118-19
Vertical Scroll bar 17
Victorians 70
Virginia Star 38

wall hangings see hangings
warm colors 9
websites 14
Wheelbarrow 125
Wild Geese Flying 54
Wild Goose Chase 54
Windows (Microsoft) 14, 16
Write 20

zig-zag designs 60
Zoom 19, 32, 34, 66

Acknowledgments

Many thanks, as always, to Alan for his help and patience.

Thanks also go to The Cotton Patch (www.cottonpatch.co.uk) and
Rio Designs (www.riodesigns.co.uk) for help with fabrics and software.